Awakening Through The Tears

Interstitial Cystitis and
The Mind/Body/Spirit Connection

CATHERINE M. SIMONE

IC Hope, Ltd.
Cleveland, Ohio

Awakening Through The Tears
Interstitial Cystitis and the Mind/Body/Spirit Connection

Copyright © 2002

IC Hope, Ltd.
First Printing 2002

ISBN 978-0-9667750-2-0

Library of Congress Control Number
2002115430

Printed in the United States by Morris Publishing
3212 East Highway 30
Kearney, NE 68847
1-800-650-7888

This book is dedicated
with undying love and gratitude
to my husband Charlie
whose love helped heal me
and led me....
gently
...back to me.

In memory of

Lee "Cory" Murphy
My very first close friend with IC

And

Latifa Atira
A true healer, a true friend

Acknowledgements

I thank God, not only for all of the miracles of my healing, but also for the courage to write these books and put myself "out there" in this way. Though I know this may sound crazy right now (I hope it doesn't sound crazy after you read this book), I also want to thank God for my IC.

A most special thank you to my husband Charlie without whom none of my books would have been written. Not only because I would not have made it physically (or in any other way really), but because of his constant support and patience as I talked endlessly about the books and what I wanted them to be. For believing in me when no one else did, for sticking up for me when I didn't have the strength, for taking as much stress out of my life as humanly possible, for listening to me complain and being there for me when I was afraid, for waking up with me in the middle of the night to give me a back rub so I could get back to sleep, for helping with all the housework and the shopping, for never complaining about dealing with a wife who has IC, for providing me *everything* I needed to heal, and most of all, for being my very best friend. Thanks for loving me no matter what.

I want to thank all of my spiritual counselors, most especially my parents. Thank you for teaching me the power of prayer, the importance of forgiveness, and the strength gained from having faith. I am ever so grateful for the example you set, not only by the way you lived your lives, but most especially for your love of each other. Thank you to Ehsida for your exceptional talent in energy release work. Thank you for helping me to release the pain and to forgive. Thank you especially for reminding me of the special magic of the universe and the power I have within me. Thank you to Cynthia for your insights, advice, and support as I was healing and as I was writing. Thank you for always reassuring me that I would be okay. Thank you to Latifa for your words of wisdom, your gentle healings, and your friendship. May you continue to rest in the loving peace of Spirit. To the authors I have read whose thoughts, teachings, and perspectives have helped to mold my own. Authors such as James Redfield, Sanaya Roman, Gary Zukov, Carolyn Myss, Louis Hay, Deepak Chopra, and most especially Neale Donald Walsch, all of whom have had the courage to come out and say what they think and write what they know to be their truths, to them I will always be grateful.

Strangely enough I would also like to thank the woman on the Internet who slandered my first book. Thank you for reminding me to send love to my "enemies", for helping me to believe even more strongly in what I had written, and for reminding me of something that is sometimes difficult to believe, that God has sent us nothing but angels. Even those who have wronged me or hurt me have served me well in the growth of my soul.

Thank you to Jane Procacci and Barb Willis for being so generous in your unwavering support of my writing and thank you most especially for your friendship.

A special thank you to my family and to Charlie's family for their patience and understanding as I worked to heal myself the rest of the way.

A most special heartfelt thank you to Simon. Thank you for your courage, inspiration, and love. You will always live on in our hearts.

Introduction

We are, all of us, looking for inner peace, for happiness, for love and approval. We are, all of us, on the same spiritual journey. Though our religions may differ and our beliefs may not be exactly the same, to me, it does not matter. In the end, I believe that all paths lead to God. I believe that our spirituality has to do with our soul and our relationship to the Divine. I don't believe our spirituality is measured by what building we go to pray in, whether a church, temple, or mosque, or even whether we choose not to go to a particular building. I don't believe that God cares what specific type of organized religious service we participate in or even whether we choose to participate in one. I believe God loves each one of us the same no matter what religion we choose to follow. And I believe that we can "find" God and be a spiritual person without ever choosing one specific religion in particular. I believe in all religions. I believe that they are all generally the same thing. They may have different stories and traditions, they may have different symbols and different man made rules, but they are all basically about the same thing. They are all about a higher power. They are all about the source of all life, the source of all goodness. They are all about love. They are all about God. Though some people find their spirituality through organized religion, spirituality itself is not about organized religion. And this book is not about organized religion either.

This book is the story of how I came to awaken spiritually while I was sick with IC and as I was healing from IC. It's about how I learned to use the fact that the mind, body, and spirit are connected in order to help me heal and how I came to understand the question that I think we all come to ask. Why me? Why is this happening to me? What did I do to deserve this? If God is up there, why is He allowing all this to happen to me? Why does it seem like He is not hearing my prayers or helping me?

I recognize that the subject of this book is a very touchy one. I think the mind/body/spirit connection is a touchy subject for people with any illness, let alone an illness where you are told that it's "all in your head" for possibly years before being diagnosed. I will do my best not to offend anyone with my personal beliefs as I truly feel respect for each individual no matter where they are on their own spiritual journey, no matter where they are on their own healing journey, or for that matter, no matter where they are in their understanding of Interstitial Cystitis.

I have no way to relate to the invasion of privacy or the expectations of the public that those who are famous in our society must endure, but I can tell you this. Once you write a book, some people expect that you are somehow different from them. For example, I spent nearly all of my time speaking with IC patients on line while I was sick. Shortly after finding an IC support group on line, I ended up becoming a co-leader. I quickly became busy trying to offer support and my own experiences, trying to help other IC patients as much as I could and often gleaning as much information and support as I was trying to share. I was always seen as "one of them" because, of course, I was. And then after my first book was published, I started receiving e-mails and phone calls from people saying things like..."did you ever cheat on the IC diet or the anti-candida diet?" or "were you ever afraid you weren't going to get better?", etc. The answer, of course, was a gigantic YES. Of course I did. I'm just like you. I am just an IC patient who was desperate to get better. Maybe I was a little more desperate with severe IC than someone who has a mild case, but still. Still I learned what I learned, figured out what I figured out, and did what I did, what I felt I had to do in order to get better, all of it solely based out of desperation. The desperation to get well and live a life free of pain and discomfort is what was driving me. No different, I'm sure, than you. I'm sure you probably feel that same desperation to get rid of IC and get back to living your life as I did which is I'm sure what has led you to my book(s).

It's been over two years since I first sat down to write this book. During these past two years, I ended up writing *Along the Healing Path* instead. After *To Wake In Tears,* I was swamped with e-mails and phone calls from IC patients looking for more help and information on how to heal from IC using a natural, holistic approach. I knew that needed to come first. So I put this book aside for a time and tried to answer their questions with *Along the Healing Path.* I'm glad to be back. I've wanted to write about the mind/body/spirit connection and healing from IC for a long time now. Actually, I've wanted to share some of this information ever since I was writing *To Wake In Tears* back in 1997-98. In some ways I felt as if I was sharing only part of the story when I wrote *To Wake In Tears.* I had only touched on and hinted at the spiritual part of my healing. I knew back then that this needed to be a separate book. Not only because there is so much to say on this subject, but also because I wasn't sure everyone would be interested in, or open to, these types of ideas. I realize now that it doesn't matter. I have never written my books for people to agree with me or to try and get on the New York Times bestsellers list. I have written my books to help IC patients find a way out of the suffering, to find their way out of the torture of IC. My first two books were about hope, healing, and empowerment. And this one is no different.

This book is for those of you curious as to how I finished healing after *To Wake In Tears,* wondering if I did in fact get the rest of the way better as I had hoped, planned, and believed. This book is for those of you wondering if I have any new insights or if I have changed my opinions of what IC is all about and how to heal from it on a physical level. This book, like my first two, is written especially for you, the IC patient. My desire is to again offer you more hope, more understanding, and some more new ideas to help you heal from IC. My desire is to empower you further with even more tools to help you heal. Again I speak openly and candidly as I share with you the rest of my story. I care only that it helps IC patients and refuse to concern myself with what is embarrassing, humiliating or risky for me to say and instead, I'm just going to say it. My desire is to share with you what I know to be true for myself. To share what I know has helped me to heal from this devastating bladder disease that can interfere with every aspect of our life. This book is about how I awakened on a spiritual level throughout my healing on a physical level. It is about how I used the fact that the mind, body, and spirit are connected in order to help me heal from severe IC. I am writing as if you have read my first two books so as not to be completely repetitive and boring. This book picks up where *To Wake In Tears* left off. I hope you find something helpful in this book that might lead you to the spiritual answers you've been looking for in regard to your own IC.

Contents

"Hope is the companion of power and mother of success; for whoso hopes strongly has within him the gift of miracles."
– Samuel Smiles

Chapter 1

---◆---

Here I Sit

As I sit here drying the tears and trying to breathe, I am astounded at the fears I still feel. It has been 4 months since *To Wake In Tears* was published. And here I sit, with pen in hand, trying to expel the fears through the ink and these words. My husband Charlie left for the Cayman Islands just minutes ago. It's a trip for work, but spouses were allowed to go. A week on the beach, alone with the love of my life...a dream I've been praying for...and yet, here I sit. I couldn't go. I'm still not ready. It breaks my heart. And Charlie, well, he loves me too much to let it show.

"Go in there and write," he said to me in the driveway as we said our last goodbyes. "Write how you feel because I'm sure others feel the same way." He gave me one last hug and got in the car. He waved goodbye yelling out the car window "Spoil yourself!", as he always tells me to do when he leaves for an extended period of time. Spoil myself. Hmmm... I'm still learning what that means.

So here I sit, writing down my feelings as the tears stream down my face. Well...I'm not sure if anyone else feels this way or not, but I can tell you that right now, I feel like a total idiot. I feel stupid and weak for feeling so afraid. I feel silly for sitting here crying and for being scared of what might happen while I'm here alone these next eight days and nights.

It's not the being alone that bothers me. I've spent countless hours alone since I was diagnosed with severe interstitial cystitis (IC). Like

1

others with more severe cases of IC, I was often housebound and sometimes bedridden with IC and the effects of IC. I missed out on a lot of the things of life. I missed family gatherings, hanging out with friends, going to concerts, playing tennis, going out to dinner…you know, normal things that people do. There were times this made me very angry and times I felt very alone. I was in my early 30's and this was NOT the way it was supposed to be. This was not at all what I had in mind.

But right now, it's not the spending time alone that's bothering me. I've actually gotten kind of used to that. In fact, in some ways, it's been a strange blessing of sorts. I ended up learning a lot about myself, about my own spirituality, and about life, by spending so much time alone. (Much of what I'm about to share with you in this book was born out of my IC enforced isolation.) In some ways, I feel like I can relate to those in solitary confinement and how they tend to grow spiritually through their time of solitude. No…it's not the being alone that's bothering me right now. It's the "not knowing what might happen to me physically" while Charlie is away. That, I know, is what I'm really afraid of.

Even though physically I am so much better than I was, there are still some symptoms that remain. Some people were under the misimpression that I was all finished healing five minutes after *To Wake In Tears* was published. This was simply not the case. Healing from IC (and the multitude of IC related symptoms and illnesses that can come with it) is no easy feat and it definitely takes time. At this point, I am still cleansing, still rebuilding, still waiting patiently (and not so patiently) to finish healing.

But that's not really why I'm sitting here. It's not why I didn't go. There are probably a lot of people out there traveling right this minute who are sicker than I am right now. Hell…I traveled when I was much more sick than I am right now. The truth is…I didn't go because I was too scared to go. I was afraid of getting really sick, being in pain, and needing, or at least wanting, to get back home right away. Home was

2

where I had things that could help and home was where at least I could be a little more comfortable. I was afraid of being in some strange bathroom with a severe IBS attack (which at this point is still one of my remaining IC related symptoms). I was afraid of getting those poison rush feelings, covered in a cold sweat, my heart pounding in my chest, severe pain in my gut, and that "going far away" feeling in my head like when you're about to pass out. But I wasn't just afraid of getting sick like that away from home, I was also afraid of getting sick like that AT home. And even more afraid when this happened during times when I was all by myself. If something went seriously wrong, if my throat closed up and I couldn't breathe from some strange allergic reaction, if my bladder started to spasm and stopped working, if the IBS got horrible and I was having trouble keeping from passing out, if I had some other weird allergic reaction to God knows what, who was I going to call? Who was going to know how to help me?

To me (and at least for me), when you have IC, there is no 911. I felt I had no one to call in an emergency situation. There was no one who was going to understand that IC is more than just a bladder disease or that my body was very toxic and therefore *extremely* sensitive. There was no one who was going to understand that my edema/swelling wasn't just fat and that it was painful to have someone touch me let alone press all over me to examine me. How would I be able to explain all my symptoms and what I was allergic to, etc., in the middle of an emergency situation? And who was going to listen to me, believe me, and understand me enough to help? Having no one to call in an emergency situation is a very scary place to live when emergency situations come on a fairly regular basis.

Some people who don't have IC or maybe even those with mild IC might be thinking, geez, it's just a bladder disease, what is this girl talking about fearing for her life for. And some people might think maybe I shouldn't say these things because maybe I'm scaring people with the truth. But for those of us with more severe IC, those of us with all the other symptoms and illnesses that can come with IC, know that I am not exaggerating in the least when I say that it seems as if our bodies are falling apart and that no one knows what to do to help. It's a scary place to be, I can tell you that. A very scary place. And a very lonely place.

You see...the loneliness of IC is not really defined by the amount of time many of us end up having to spend alone because we are too sick to go places and do things. It is not the amount of time alone that is as hard as the loneliness of no one understanding how we feel, the loneliness of no one understanding IC. There is a deep aloneness in the physical pain of IC. There is a deep aloneness in the incredibly uncomfortable, never-ending urgency. And there is an extra deep aloneness in the fact that often, for IC patients, no one is really showing much concern over our pain and symptoms. For many of us, there is a gigantic lack of compassion, sympathy and understanding from family, friends, and doctors. And that HUGE lack of compassion, sympathy, and understanding can have a tremendously huge impact on our emotional well-being, our physical healing, and how incredibly alone we feel in our fears and in our pain.

I know so many IC patients who have said things like "it would have been much easier to have cancer than to have IC". I even know IC patients who have had cancer AND IC and they have all said that IC is worse. Every single one of them has said that. And why? Because it's worse to have a disease that no one has ever heard of, that no one understands, and that no one cares all that much about it. It's worse because when you have IC, most people don't understand how much you are suffering physically. They show you very little compassion or concern and in some cases, they just plain don't even believe that you have anything physically wrong with you. I know parents who don't believe their child or teenager really has a physical disease and therefore the child or teenager's suffering is not only shown no regard, but they are treated as if they are "doing this on purpose" or as if it's "in their head". Obviously this doesn't just happen to children and teenagers, which is tragic enough. There are plenty of adults whose spouses and family act as if IC is the person's fault, like the person wants to be sick or isn't even sick. At the least, they act as if it's no big deal. Sometimes family members refuse to read about it, hear about it, or make any attempt at understanding it. And if the IC patient tries to get them to understand, they are often met with coldness. When you are diagnosed with something like cancer, it is highly unlikely that you will get this type of response.

For me, the whole "no one understanding IC" was a HUGE thing. It was very difficult for me to get over it on an emotional level. Realizing that people who I thought cared about me really didn't care was very hard. Realizing that people who had known me my whole entire life to be a reasonable, intelligent, levelheaded person now thought I was crazy or that it was "all in my head" was very upsetting to me. I was very hurt by the people in my life that I thought would "be there for me", because they definitely weren't. However, I was extremely fortunate to have Charlie, my sister-in-law Sue, and my mom who were there for me the whole way through. I know some IC patients who don't even have one person who is there for them through their IC nightmare. This makes me so very sad because I know how incredibly awful it feels and how incredibly lonely. Sometimes the whole "no one understanding IC" was almost as upsetting as having IC to begin with. Well…almost.

Why does it have to be so hard? Why couldn't we have gotten a disease that somebody knows something about? A disease that people in our families and in our lives have heard of even? Why did we have to get IC? I can't imagine a person with IC who hasn't asked these kinds of questions.

It's one thing when family and friends don't understand what we're going through, but it's a whole other thing that many doctors don't either. It's one thing to feel alone emotionally and another to feel alone in your physical pain and symptoms because most doctors have little understanding of what we are really going through. Many doctors have no concept of the physical pain that some IC patients experience nor do they consider that their other "weird" symptoms have anything to do with their IC. Many doctors still don't "believe in" IC, as if a physical disease is something to be "believed in". And even if they do believe that IC is a real disease, some still don't believe the pain is as bad as it actually is. Therefore many IC patients suffer MUCH more than they should have to because they are not treated for their pain the way a cancer patient would be. A cancer patient is believed when they have pain and they are given something to help alleviate it. They are not treated like they are crazy or too emotional. They are not treated as if they were drug addicts looking for a fix. They are treated, as we should also be, as if they have a physical disease with physical symptoms and real pain. When you have a disease that people have heard of, a disease that they know something about and can relate to, you get much more compassion, sympathy, and understanding from family, friends, and doctors. You don't get treated as if it is all your fault that you're sick. Instead, you get the emotional (and physical) support that you need to help you heal (at least in most cases). With IC, many of us don't. Many of us live in a very different reality.

I'll tell you this. I've never cried so often. I've never been so scared. I've never been in as much physical pain and I've never felt so alone as when I was sick with IC. The trauma I went through was something I could never have imagined would have happened to me. I can't believe that I made it through all the pain, infection, and poison to come out on the other end and be okay. Though I have to admit, I didn't come out of it without any scars. There is no doubt I still have some. I sit here hoping that they will begin to heal as I write this book.

I think for me, the fear started that very first night in the recovery room, that very first night that my bladder wouldn't work. The first time I felt the burning, the stinging, the cramping, and the pain. The first night that I felt the panic that I think anyone would feel the minute they realized that something was terribly wrong with their body and they didn't know what to do about it. I know that my fear grew throughout that first year when I was still trying to get diagnosed. During that time I was being told that my bladder bleeding and not working properly was "all in my head" and it scared the you know what out of me knowing that something was horribly wrong with me physically and no one could see it! My fear multiplied several times over once I was finally diagnosed and came to realize that the doctors really couldn't help me. And then it grew to gigantic proportions as I continued to try and get help from others (alternative doctors, healers, etc.) and got hurt even more. As more and more symptoms kept popping up that I had no idea what to do about, the more afraid I became. And though there were many times that I was scared from the pain and the mystery of my symptoms, believe it or not, my fear hadn't turned to total overall anxiety and occasional "panic attacks" until I was physically almost completely better, nearly four years later.

It's such a challenge to not be hard on myself for feeling this way. I keep telling myself that with all I have been through, all the traumatic experiences in the last four years, I have a right to come out of it with some fears and anxieties. I'm only human after all. The question was...how was I going to get rid of them? I had to be able to go through my days without fear and anxiety about what else might happen to me health-wise. Charlie is probably right. Maybe other IC patients, as they get better (or even while they're not) have these same types of fears, these same types of feelings.

As I sit here disappointed that I'm not going with Charlie, I realize how hard it's been the past four years. Having severe IC and dozens of other symptoms has really taken its toll on me. Being so sick and not knowing what to do to get better, being in pain most of the time, having no control over more things going wrong with my body, and not knowing what to do about it when they did, had me in a constant state of high stress. I lived in that fight or flight mode most all the time when I was sick. I could tell that I was running on adrenaline. I barely got any sleep with getting up to go to the bathroom twenty times a night and being in pain all the time, yet somehow I always seemed to be awake. I was rarely tired in a "normal" way. I couldn't allow myself to be. I had to stay on top of things because if I didn't help myself, who would? If I didn't read and research about IC and all the related symptoms I had, how was I going to figure it out and be able to get better? I had no choice. I stayed awake and alert for survival. I stayed in that fight or flight mode out of necessity. And now, even though physically I am so much better, I am left with this anxiety, this fear of getting really sick and having no one there to help me. It's as if I've run out of courage. I feel as if I've lost my nerve. Actually, what I've really lost is my sense of well-being. I've lost the confidence that my body will be okay.

How did I get here? How did I get to a place where no one could understand what was physically wrong with me? Having IC has changed my body so much. My body has become SO SENSITIVE and somehow that has made me so different from other "normal" healthy people; so different that I feel I can't even go to the emergency room when something goes wrong or even to any doctor (medical or alternative) without the risk of being hurt by them accidentally.

Being afraid of getting sick and having no one there who understands, believes me, or can help me is only one of the fears that developed with my IC. Another huge fear that I acquired was the fear of being trapped. Whether in a traffic jam, a dentist's chair, or somewhere in public where the line is long or there is no public restroom. Anywhere where I felt trapped without easy access to a bathroom caused major anxiety. And because a delay in getting to a bathroom would cause additional pain and more symptoms (and of course the threat of a possible accident) it was a situation I tried to avoid as much as possible. I know many IC patients who are afraid of being trapped without a bathroom. I knew this was a "normal" fear or anxiety-producing situation for those of us with IC. I also know that due to the fact that most IC patients develop all kinds of allergies and sensitivities to foods, medications, herbs, etc., that many of us have a fear of trying new things. I know that personally I had several horrible (some life threatening) experiences due to allergic reactions and they were all to things that I wasn't allergic to prior to getting IC so they all seemed to me to come out of the blue. This great uncertainty of what can hurt you BADLY can make trying new things and even using/eating things you're used to using/eating, very scary. I know several IC patients that are afraid to leave the safety of their home (and their bathroom) or are afraid to go places alone or places far from their house. And even though I knew this was "normal" for having been through all that we go through, I still never imagined that I would become this way. I don't know why I thought I was immune to feeling this type of anxiety and fear. I guess it's because I was never what someone would call a nervous type of person.

As I sit here, I remember what I used to be like before I got sick. Before I ever got IC, I was so different. I was brave and strong, not really afraid of much of anything that I can remember. I suppose I was afraid of dying if I had ever thought much about it, but I rarely ever did. I had some type of inner confidence where I knew that no matter what happened, I could deal with it. I was always an athletic, active type of person with a job and a "life". Then I got IC and I changed. I became vulnerable because I was so sick. I became scared in a way that I never had been scared before. My experience of life changed so much. It became physically painful and physically unpredictable. I never knew when my bladder would work or when it wouldn't. And if it did work, I never knew when it would be excruciatingly painful or just mildly uncomfortable. I never knew if I would ever get any sleep or if I was going to be awake, alone in the bathroom all night. I never knew if when I went to the doctor whether they would know what was wrong or know what to do about it. I never knew if they would even believe me or if they would just think I was some crazy, emotional female. I never knew how I would feel from one day to the next or even from one hour to the next. What I thought was so, was no longer so. What I thought I could count on, I could no longer count on. What I used to take for granted, I no longer even had. Things like my job, certain friends, my physical strength, and my general health; all the way down to my ability to perform such a normal (and necessary I might add) everyday

9

bodily function as going to the bathroom, they all became things of the past. Being so sick with a disease that is not only poorly understood by the doctors and everyone else in your life but is also a disease that can affect every area of your life (no sex, nothing good to eat, can't get away from the bathroom, feel miserable most of the time), it can really take it's toll emotionally. Eventually, somewhere along the line, I became someone who was afraid to go places. Not because I thought the place I was going to was a scary place, but because I was afraid of a possible traffic jam on the highway on the way there (where there was no way to get to a bathroom quick). I was afraid of something horrible happening to me physically that I had no control over. Something that came out of the blue, something that I could not stop from happening. I was afraid because that kind of thing happened to me quite often when my IC was severe and even along the way as I was getting better. I was like many IC patients who become chemically sensitive with multiple allergies. Being so sensitive to things like exhaust fumes, cigarette smoke, perfume, cleaning supplies, anything at all that was chemical or toxic, made me even more nervous to go places because I didn't know what I would be exposed to or how sick I would become after being exposed. I became someone who was afraid of not having my husband around because he was the only one who really understood what I had gone through physically and the only one who I felt could help me when something else went wrong. What I became was someone who was afraid to go to the Cayman Islands on vacation. And that's why I'm sitting here writing to you now.

Why is this happening to me?! I sit here frustrated and angry, asking the same question I've been asking since the first night my IC symptoms began. No matter how much I've tried to look on the bright side and have a good attitude, no matter how much I realize that, of course, much worse things can happen to a person, it's still hard to get away from this question. Why me? Why is this happening to me?!

And now it seems I have a whole new battle to fight. These fears and the anxiety I'm feeling have gotten totally out of control. I have to figure this out. I can't live my life like this. I can't be afraid whenever Charlie isn't around. I can't be scared to leave the house or get on an airplane because what if I get sick and need to be in the bathroom for an extended period of time. It's so hard not to wonder why this is happening now. After all this struggling to heal my bladder and get well physically and now I'm going to be left with THIS?! No way will I accept that. I know I will get back to my old confident self even though I have absolutely no idea how I will get there. Who knows…maybe it just hasn't sunk in yet that physically I'm almost all better…? The fact is I do still have some symptoms. And because they still remain somewhat unpredictable and I still can't be totally sure that I don't have any strange allergies left, maybe that's why I'm still afraid…? I don't know. Whatever the reasons, I can hardly believe this is me. If anyone had ever tried to tell me that I would ever feel this way, I would never have believed it. Not in a million years would I have ever believed it.

And yet, here I sit.

Two Years Later...

Chapter 2

This Isn't Me

They say that God only gives a person as much as he or she can handle. This must be true because if I were petrified like this the whole time I was sick, I don't think I would have made it. As sick as I was with all the IC related symptoms, as much as my bladder was raw and bleeding, as much as I was afraid from how bad I felt physically, somehow it's not the same thing as the fear I've been feeling these past couple years.

It feels so strange to me to be this afraid. I just don't feel like myself. Actually, I haven't felt like myself since my IC began. But somehow I thought that when I got better physically, that I would automatically start to feel like myself again. And in some ways I did, but in one way, I definitely didn't. It's like when I was first diagnosed with IC this also feels very overwhelming. And just like when I was first diagnosed with IC, I have no idea what to do to get better. Again (or should I say still) I feel incredibly vulnerable and afraid of being hurt further, whether by someone else "doing something to me" (or trying to convince me to take something) or even (or should I say especially) by something new going wrong with my body. Even though physically I am better, I still don't have back the confidence that my body is now going to be okay.

Healing from IC, at least for me, has never been straightforward. I was always getting better with one thing and then having some new symptom to deal with. It was often one step forward, two steps back. Getting better has been a slow and unpredictable road with mystery, discomfort, and pain along the way. (I know, stop trying to cheer you up...right?) All of the things I was using to help me get better from the IC (and IC related) symptoms, all of the various herbs, natural products, and "alternative" treatments that I told you about in my first two books, were definitely NOT being used to treat IC at the time. Actually, they still aren't. And even though many IC patients are now trying a more natural approach to healing, back when I was trying to get better, I had no one to talk to about the things I was doing/using to help me heal. Even though at the time, I was speaking with hundreds of IC patients via the Internet, no one I knew of was doing any of the things I was doing. Most people were using the standard medical treatments (e.g., bladder instillations, medications) or were trying long-term antibiotics at the time. All of my IC friends, I'm sure, thought I was more than a little bit crazy with what I was doing. At the time, no one had ever heard of drinking marshmallow root tea, taking herbal baths, cleansing and detoxing the body, doing NAET treatments, or having their mercury fillings replaced, in order to help heal from IC. At the time, there was no one to talk to about what I was doing or how it was working, etc. This definitely made things a lot scarier and a lot more stressful. I really had to learn to listen to my body and to my gut instincts or intuition, and I had to learn to trust both. This was made even more difficult by the fact that I just didn't feel like myself most of the time.

It's hard to feel like yourself when you're sick and when you have to stop participating in so much of life (both work and pleasure). In so many ways we can lose our identity and our dignity when we're sick. And of course having a more embarrassing, not very well known disease doesn't help. Not only do we have to go to the bathroom all the time (which can interfere with virtually any activity) often it takes us a long time in the bathroom due to a weak urine stream and/or difficulty initiating the stream. Aside from the embarrassment, which of course some people feel more than others, some IC patients are too sick to work and have to go on disability. Even those with IC who can still work or go to school often have to miss out on a lot of extra curricular activities. Speaking of extra curricular activities, for many IC patients, having sex is difficult, if not impossible. When you have IC, it can be tough to enjoy things the way you used to. When my IC was bad, and even as I was getting better, it was difficult to all the way feel like myself because a lot of the time my mind was on how I was feeling physically. I really couldn't help it. I don't know if you feel that way or not, but for me, the ever-present urgency, the pain, the discomfort of having so many things wrong with my body at the same time, it was hard to think of much else.

I also didn't feel like myself because I could no longer dress the way I used to. I had the usual IC bloating or swelling in the pelvic area where you look like you're three months pregnant, so I couldn't wear any of my normal clothes. I had to wear clothes that were loose fitting around the waist or my symptoms would all increase dramatically. I also had the lovely symptom of edema (swelling all over my body) that also came with my IC (though a bit later) and that also made me feel huge and not like myself. I had to stop wearing a bra even before I got the edema because it just hurt way too much to have one on. Not that I was ever big on wanting to wear one, but it does inhibit the clothes you can wear when you don't. It was just way too uncomfortable to have anything squeezing me anywhere, socks, bras, underwear, pants, it didn't matter what. It was more than uncomfortable; it was actually painful. I also stopped wearing make-up (not that I ever wore all that much, but I did wear some). I wasn't really going anywhere or seeing anyone the majority of the time, so I just didn't bother. All of these things combined made me feel icky, ugly, bloated, and just plain gross. So I didn't feel like myself or look like myself when I was sick.

But things have changed so much. Physically I am so much better it's astounding. I really don't have half the reasons to be afraid that I used to and yet sometimes I would swear that I am even more afraid now. It's so hard for me not to blame myself for not being strong enough, not being brave enough, not being able to handle all this. I'm not sure right now what all this fear is really about. I feel there is much more to it than what I am aware of right now. I do feel like it has something to do with me writing this book, but somehow that's not making me feel any better right now.

I remember that it was only a couple of weeks after Charlie returned home from the Cayman Islands that it was Mother's Day. We were to drive over to see my mom and the rest of my family for a visit. My mom was now living in my grandmother's condo because my grandmother had passed away several months before and because my mom's lease had just ended so it made sense for her to move in there. I hadn't been over to my grandma's since she died and I definitely hadn't been there since my mom had moved in. There was no question that I was a little nervous to go there. I was nervous to see my mom living there, my grandma not there, and really just to have to face the reality of the situation. On our way there is when it happened. I started to not feel too good. It was that same familiar, horrible feeling of intestinal spasms and pain, being covered in a cold sweat, feeling like I was about to throw up and go to the bathroom at the same time (like when you drink too much alcohol or have the flu really bad), and feeling that old familiar IC panic of knowing I needed to get to the bathroom quick. Fortunately this happened when we were only a few minutes from our house. Still, I barely made it back in time. Now that I look back, I can see that this was really the beginning. It was the beginning of my "fear of going far away from the house"/anxiety/panic attack type symptom. This happening, the getting sick like that in the car and wondering if I'd make it back home in time, though I didn't realize it at the time, marked some kind of change in me. Yes the fears had been there all along and yes I was nervous to go places when I was sick with IC, but not like this. Not like this AT ALL. Now it was totally different. Suddenly it turned into something else, something new.

Actually, now that I think about it, this wasn't *completely* new. I had gotten sick like that every time I went to the dentist the year prior. With each appointment to have my mercury fillings replaced, I would get so incredibly nervous to be "trapped" in the chair; the shot of Novocain making it feel even more like I was stuck there and had to get it done

18

no matter how I felt. The night before each appointment I would get very little sleep anticipating what would happen the next morning. Then the morning of the appointment I would feel really sick like I had the flu, with diarrhea and throwing up and just feeling incredibly awful in general. Of course the dentist I went to was thirty minutes across town (close to where I used to live) so it was a nightmare trying to get there with all the bathroom stops along the way. I remember I would barely breathe in the car on the way there because I was so afraid. It's a miracle that I made it through those appointments. It wasn't easy for me or for Charlie who (God bless him) would somehow get me there with all the complaining and bathroom stops along the way and then he would even hold my hand through the whole appointment because I was such a nervous wreck. But with the dentist, I could understand more why I was nervous with the whole fear of being trapped in the chair thing and also the fear of having someone "doing something to me" that also developed while I was sick from having some really bad experiences with the doctors. But to be that nervous to go visit my family at a place where I've been a hundred times before, where no one was going to touch me or hurt me physically, and where I wasn't trapped in any way…this was strange to me. This was the first time that the fear or anticipation of emotional pain seemed to elicit the same response in my body as the fear of being hurt physically.

Shortly after this "straw that broke the camels back" incident on mothers day, I began shying away from going places, afraid that this would happen again. And it did happen again, many times actually. Whenever I would get really nervous it would happen. And the other variable that made me even more afraid and even more confused as to what the cause was, this could also happen at anytime. I didn't HAVE to be nervous for it to happen. It happened in the middle of the night where I would wake up and be sick like that. It happened sometimes in the mornings shortly after waking up, especially around my menstrual cycle. And it happened sometimes for no apparent reason when I was at home and totally relaxed. So this great mystery of when it was going to happen did not help AT ALL and definitely added to my anxiety level and fear of going places. Gradually, over about a year's time, I became so afraid to go places that were far away from my house (or really anywhere where I thought I could be trapped without easy access to a bathroom) that I pretty much stopped going.

I didn't have agoraphobia. It wasn't really like that. I wasn't afraid of going places or being with other people. It wasn't the places or the people. It was the not knowing when I was going to get totally sick with diarrhea, vomiting (sometimes I just felt like I was going to, but didn't), and that "going far away in my head" feeling that on one hand was so very familiar to me from when I was really sick with the IC and IBS and yet, it was still just as scary each time it happened. That feeling is what I was really afraid of the most. (I think.) And I didn't have normal panic attacks either. I didn't have the usual symptoms that people get with panic attacks where you feel like you can't breathe or like you're going to have a heart attack. But I did feel a sense of panic when the symptoms would start. I would panic that I had to get to a bathroom yes, but I would also be freaking out and afraid about the "going far away in my head" feeling because it felt like I was going to literally die each time. So I did feel a sense of panic inside. Another difference I had between agoraphobia and classic panic attacks was, for me, there really was no "safety zone". Usually people feel better when they are at home in their "safety zone" and they are only afraid when they leave the "safety" of their house. For me, the same fear/anxiety/panic feeling could be there when I was at home just as easily as when I wasn't. As soon as I would get a wave of feeling sick, a "poison rush" feeling as I used to call it, as soon as I would get covered in a thin layer of cold sweat, as soon as I felt that familiar feeling in my intestines, I would feel a wave of panic, which I believe would then make things even worse. The anxiety or panic feelings would bring the symptoms on even further. And so it was a sort of cycle once things got started. If I were nervous, it would start the physical symptoms and if the physical symptoms started even when I wasn't nervous, then I would *become* nervous and it would get even worse. This was so upsetting to me because I felt that I should somehow be able to control this from happening. I knew that being nervous made it worse, but once I felt bad physically, I just couldn't help but be afraid. And sometimes I couldn't help being nervous about going somewhere and then that would also cause the symptoms to start. So naturally I was blaming myself. Even though I knew that this could happen regardless of how I felt nervous-wise, I still felt somehow I should be able to control this fear/anxiety/panic feeling.

It is so frustrating and embarrassing to be this way. As if it wasn't bad enough to have had IC where people couldn't see it or understand it, now I have to tell people "I'm better physically, but I still can't go places or do things"! This is nuts! It was hard enough asking family and friends to understand when I was terribly sick. I couldn't help but worry about how they were going to understand *this*. And it makes me angry with myself that I even care what they're going to think, but I can't help it. To top it all off, here I was with a master's degree and a license to counsel other people and I couldn't even help myself. All the positive thinking and positive self-talk were not even touching this. Everything I knew to do in terms of how I would help someone else deal with his or her anxiety wasn't helping me one bit. It was as if my intellect and my body were not connected. For example, even when, intellectually, I knew for certain that there was nothing to be afraid of, it was like my body wasn't hearing me. It was still reacting in a panic. My nerves, it felt, were making me physically sick. Here I could eat whatever I wanted, both bladder-wise and IBS-wise, and I would have no symptoms to speak of. But tell me I have to go get my haircut or go to the dentist for a teeth cleaning and there I would be, stuck in the bathroom, sick as a dog. It was like, somewhere along the way as I was healing from IC and everything else, I became allergic to being nervous.

I just didn't feel like myself. Even though I was SO much better physically than when my IC was severe, I *still* couldn't go places comfortably and enjoy myself. Along the way everyone was telling me things like "it's to be expected after everything I went through" to feel this anxiety. And for a while I tried to tell myself the same thing. But there is more to it than that. I know there is. I'm more afraid now than I was when I had every reason to be afraid. There *has* to be a reason. This just isn't me!

I was just as shocked and perplexed with this new anxiety symptom as I was when I first got IC. I wanted to know, I *needed* to know, why this was happening to me...how this could possibly be happening to me?! I needed to know how it happened not just on a physical level, but on a spiritual level as well. Why was God allowing this to happen to me? Why was it necessary for the growth of my soul to be this afraid?

It looked as if healing the rest of the way was going to be just as much of a challenge as it was to get this far. But I won't give up now. Not when I'm this close.

"Learn to get in touch with the silence within yourself
and know that everything in life has a purpose."
– Elisabeth Kubler-Ross

Chapter 3

---◆---

It's Not Our Fault

I think it's normal to wonder why. I think it's normal to, at times, be angry or depressed that we got IC and I think it's normal to wonder why this is all happening to us. It's normal and just plain human for our thoughts to go there. And it's normal for our prayers to reflect our frustration and confusion. Maybe you have found yourself at times wondering why you have been "chosen" to get IC, why you are having to experience the lack of understanding and concern from others, why you are having to suffer with all these physical symptoms. Maybe you have wondered why you now have to live with the limitations, the stress, the inconvenience and the pain that IC has brought into your life. If you have asked any or all of these questions, I hope you know that you are totally normal for doing so.

Understanding how we got IC on a physical level is difficult enough. To this day, not much about IC has been scientifically proven. There is no scientifically proven cause and no known medical cure. With the cause of IC unproven and the still fairly pervasive attitude of doubt shared by many in the medical profession even today as to the realities of this disease, it can leave even the most confident of us wondering, did WE somehow cause this to happen? Is there something we did that made us get IC? Why did this happen to us?

We are all trying to find the cause of our IC. Both physically and spiritually, we wonder how we got it and why. Some people blame themselves. Whether they think they dieted too excessively, drank too much alcohol or diet soda, had too much stress, or whatever, some people (even if only privately) blame themselves for getting IC. Some people blame the doctors. Whether they think they got IC from taking too many antibiotics, from some type of female or abdominal surgery, from a catheter, from a hospital borne infection, or whatever, some people blame the doctors for giving them IC. Some people blame abuse. Whether they were sexually abused as a child or physically, verbally or sexually abused within an adult relationship. Some people blame some form of abuse for their getting IC. There are a multitude of physical reasons that people can attribute their IC to. Whether it be hormonal changes due to birth control pills, pregnancy, menopause or a hysterectomy, whether it be repeated bladder infections, some type of lingering bladder infection, systemic candida (yeast), back problems, thyroid disease, or autoimmune disease, there are so many theories as to the cause of IC. Maybe you are like me and at some point have blamed nearly all of those reasons for why you got IC.

Often in asking "why me?" on a more spiritual level, we blame ourselves. So many of us deal with guilt about being sick. It's especially hard to have an invisible disease like IC that no one understands. You feel even guiltier to take the time you need to heal, even guiltier to say "no" to doing things with or for other people because to other people, many of us look fine. They can't see our IC. As I've said before, the irony of the name IC is that no one can see it. They can't see inside our bodies into our bladders to see the inflammation, the raw spots, and the bleeding. They can't feel the pain and they certainly aren't in the bathroom with us where we usually do most of our suffering. So we end up feeling even guiltier because we know that they don't understand. And we feel (even if only subconsciously) that we don't deserve the same rights in terms of healing that people with visible (or more well known) illnesses have. Whether it's asking for pain medication, asking for time off work, taking the time for ourselves for sleep or rest, or whatever it is that will help us to heal, we often don't ask for it and we often don't take it. We feel guilty for taking it. And we don't feel justified in asking for it. I think many of us don't take the time we need to heal because we look "normal" to other people and we're scared that "they" (the doctors, our employers, our spouses, family, etc.) will not understand or believe us. Maybe they will think less of us. Maybe they will think that we are being weak, lazy, or exaggerating our symptoms. These are normal concerns, by the way, because many people DO think this of us.

Heck, we even blame ourselves on a fairly regular basis for somehow increasing our symptoms. Whether by something we ate, by how much we stressed out about something, or even because we waited too long to go to the bathroom or pushed too hard while we were trying to go, so many of us blame ourselves when we experience an increase in our symptoms. We know certain things will aggravate our IC, like having sex or eating chocolate, yet sometimes we can't help but do them. It's only normal. But we blame ourselves for that too. We know stress can increase our symptoms but it's so hard to eliminate all of our stress. It's only normal to have some stressful things going on in our lives. But when we do feel stress about these situations, we still blame ourselves for feeling it because we know it is making us feel worse physically. And then of course many times there are people who try to make us feel like it's our fault that we're sick. Doctors have told many of us that it's "all in our head" and that if we would just think differently or ignore it, that our IC would go away. Not just doctors, but maybe other people in our lives have also said or implied similar things. Even though when you have IC, you know how insanely ridiculous that is. We know that IC is a very physical disease and that no ignoring it or thinking differently is going to cure it. Still, some of us find a way to blame ourselves or feel guilty for being sick.

I know many IC patients who were told for years that their physical symptoms were "in their head". And I know some who have even believed it, at least for a time. They blamed themselves for not only getting sick, but some have also believed that they aren't EVEN sick. The fact that they have to urinate frequently, feel pain in the pelvic and bladder area, pain with intercourse, constant urgency feelings, and possibly numerous other symptoms...none of this has anything to do with it. They blame themselves for causing ALL of it. Sometimes when they have symptoms, they don't even know if they should believe what they are feeling physically. They think...am I causing this by simply being "neurotic", by hating my spouse or hating sex, by *thinking* about peeing too much, by just not thinking "right", or by being emotionally weak? Sadly, some doctors are still making these types of comments to their patients. Even sadder is that some patients believe them. We are so trained in our society to "listen to the doctor" that even when the diagnosis is "it's all in your head", we still believe them over what we are feeling in our own bodies. Hopefully with time and more accurate information about IC, this will stop happening. But for now, this can still happen to a fairly large percentage of people with "difficult to diagnose" (and difficult to treat) illnesses such as IC.

Some people are insulted by the mind/body/spirit "stuff" because they feel it is yet another way that they are being blamed for being sick. I don't blame them one bit because that's pretty much how I felt too. My first exposure to the mind/body/spirit connection after being diagnosed with IC was through the herbologist woman I mentioned in my first two books. Aside from the fact that she sold me a ton of vitamins and herbs that she said my body was "asking for" through kinesiology (muscle testing) that ended up totally making me sick, and aside from the fact that she told me that she didn't want to hear one thing about IC before prescribing all these natural supplements, this woman also decided to analyze me right there on the spot. She told me that to have bladder problems meant that you were "pissed off", that you were angry about something. She tried to tell me that I was angry with my dad for dying the year before. And to her, this was the reason why I was sick. Of course, I totally disagreed with her rookie psychological assessment of me because I knew that I wasn't angry with my dad. She had no idea how I view death or how I felt emotionally about...well anything really. This was just her simplistic judgment of why I had IC and instead of helping to enlighten me about the connection between my mind, body, and spirit, I was totally unimpressed and insulted. Besides, I really didn't *feel* angry. At least I didn't think I did.

I'm not sure if I was more insulted by the doctors that said my bladder bleeding was "all in my head" or by this herbologist lady who felt it was all my fault for being angry. Her viewpoint of why I was sick was just as insulting really. I felt like she was saying that if only I were psychologically stronger, I wouldn't be sick. As if she was saying, if I wasn't so emotionally immature and angry with my father for dying, then my bladder would not have ulcers in it and it would not be bleeding and hurting. And so I thought, in other words, what she was telling me was, if I would just "get over it" and not be angry with my dad, then I would be just fine and my bladder symptoms would magically disappear. What a bunch of hooey I thought.

Sadly, I think this is the way many people get introduced to the viewpoint that the mind, body, and spirit are connected. They run into some idiot who gives them a rookie analysis of their personality and/or life situation and then tells them that THAT is why they are sick. I want to tell you something. NO ONE can tell you why you have IC. Only YOU can know that. And I think we feel bad enough for having IC that we don't need someone telling us that it's all our fault that we are sick, that if we would just think differently that we would magically get better.

It's not your fault you have IC! You didn't do it on purpose. You didn't cause it to happen. You didn't *want* to be sick. And I know that even if you did want to be sick, you certainly wouldn't have picked IC as the disease to get. No one in their right mind would have EVER have picked IC. And by the way, it's not your fault that other people don't understand IC either. Just because they don't understand what we're going through doesn't mean we have to feel unjustified in asking for what we need in order to heal. We have to not care that they don't understand. And we have to remember that unless you have IC, it's very hard to understand it. Even if there is a person in our life who loves us and is trying as hard as they can to understand what we're going through, it's still near impossible for them to really "get it" unless they have IC and can feel what it feels like to have it. Even if someone has had a horrible bladder infection before (or saw Tom Hanks in the movie The Green Mile when he had a horrible bladder infection), they still can only understand *part* of what IC is like for so many of us. Whether people understand it or not, we have to remember always, that IC is a very physical disease with very physical causes and it is *not* our fault we got it.

If it were simply mind over matter or conscious wishing, then I would have been better the very first day; the very first minutes I was sick. It is a rare individual, I would think, that consciously wishes to be sick. But subconsciously or on a spiritual level, one that I wasn't at all aware of, I wondered, *did* I have something to do with it? Did I somehow cause myself to get sick without even realizing it?

I knew one thing. I was willing to do anything to get better. If all these people throughout history (and of course in the present) were telling me that the connection between my mind, body, and spirit could somehow help me to get well, no matter what was physically wrong with me...I was definitely going to look into it. As my friend Barb Willis and I used to say, if someone would have told us that standing on our head for 10 hours a day would cure IC, we would do it. And we wouldn't complain about it either. We'd be thrilled for an answer, thrilled for a way out of the hell that living with IC can be. So if a little self reflection was called for in order for me to either buy into or discount this whole mind/body/spirit thing, I was willing to be open minded and give it a shot.

After learning more about it, I realized that it was just another tool to help me get better. The mind/body/spirit connection is not the new age-y, "out there" concept that I had once thought. In fact, more and more medical studies are showing a strong connection between emotional health, spiritual health and physical disease. Most people today recognize that we are mind, body, and spirit. Now does this mean that our thoughts, our emotions and our soul have something to do with our having IC? Well, this was what I was going to find out.

But of course, when I first got sick, my mind was only on the physical. The getting out of the pain and misery of all my symptoms was all I could think about. The last thing on my mind was the spiritual or emotional reasons that might be involved in my being sick. At the time, my mind was not open to the spiritual aspects of illness and as I've said, I was quite insulted by the thought. When you first get diagnosed or even when you are still in the throws of all the miserable physical symptoms of IC, it is difficult to care about the spiritual or emotional reasons that may have contributed to your getting sick in the first place. And you know what? It's really not the time. Dealing with the physical symptoms must come first. Whether you choose to use medical or alternative treatments for your IC, getting out of pain and finding at least some relief from your symptoms must come first.

"To make the right choices in life, you have to get in touch with your soul. To do this, you need to experience solitude, which most people are afraid of, because in the silence you hear the truth and know the solutions."
– Deepak Chopra

Chapter 4

◆

Choices

I decided early on that I was going to take a very active role in my healing and I'll tell you this, it wasn't because I *wanted* to, it was because I felt like I had no choice. Based on all the facts, or should I say, all the unknowns with IC, I felt I had to be the one to do the research, talk to others with IC, and decide for myself what to do. I had to take responsibility for my own healing because I knew that no one else could or would be able to do it for me. Everything I did and everything I thought about back then had to do with my healing. I was determined to get my life back. I had more than just hope that I would get better. I actually *believed* that I would. After all, as silly as this might sound, my parents had always told me that I could do whatever I set my mind to. And I definitely set my mind on healing.

When I was growing up, every time I got into trouble, my dad would always talk to me about my attitude. If I was arguing with my mom or fighting with my brothers because they were teasing me or whatever it was, he would always end up talking to me about my attitude. No matter what the topic, no matter what reason I was "in trouble"; the conversation always went back to my attitude. When I was very young, I had no idea what my dad was talking about. It was frustrating because I felt like he was blaming me for whatever it was that had happened. I probably said the normal things that little kids say like… "It wasn't my fault." or "But I didn't DO anything!" (And I probably said them in some stupid, whiny kid's voice too…ugh, my poor dad.) Anyway, it wasn't until I got a little older that I started to understand what he was talking about. He was always trying to teach me that I had a choice. I had a choice about how I was going to view things, how I was going to react to things, how I was going to think about, and therefore, feel about things. It was up to me he would say. If I changed my attitude, I could change the whole situation. For example, when I was still pretty young, my dad used to tell me that it was my choice whether I was going to let my brothers' teasing bother me or not. It took some time I'm sure, but at some point I tried his suggestion. Much to my surprise, the less I let it bother me, the less they would do it (probably because then it wasn't nearly as fun for them). But there was even more to it than that, I just didn't understand it at the time. I also had a choice, he told me, whether I was going to allow someone else to hurt my feelings or not, whether I was going to feel guilty about something or not, and whether I was going to be happy or not. It was up to me if I was going to walk around in a bad mood, with a chip on my shoulder (as my dad used to say) or if I was going to be happy. Being happy was a choice he taught me. It wasn't just a feeling. And, according to my dad, I had the power to choose that feeling whenever I desired, regardless of the actual situation I was in. As frustrating as it must have been for my dad as he was trying teach me that "attitude is everything" and that my thoughts were influencing my reality, it was worth every second to him I know, because I took these concepts and lessons with me through the rest of my life. They were so successfully driven into my head (thank you Dad) that I have them there with me at the very most important moments.

One of those moments happened just a few days after I got diagnosed. And though it has been nearly seven years, I can still remember it as if it were yesterday. There I was, sitting on the toilet, rocking back and forth in agony, trying to squeeze out even a couple drops of burning hot urine as I watched blood, instead of urine, drip from my bladder. My next doctor appointment was 6 weeks away and I had only a few days left of pain medication. Sitting there in agony, I was so afraid. But not only afraid, I was also furious. I was so appalled that people were living like this and that no one seemed to care. No one seemed to be doing anything to help! This was an absolutely inhumane way to live, completely intolerable and totally torturous. I was so frustrated, angry, and in so much pain. I'll never forget what I said that day or how I said it. Charlie was waiting patiently for me outside the bathroom door (as he has done thousands of times since) to make sure I was okay. Between my teeth, in the most firm and determined voice I could muster, I said to him "I am going to figure this out. I am going to get better and then I am going to write a book to help other people get better." Two and a half years later I wrote *To Wake In Tears: Understanding Interstitial Cystitis*.

That moment was so powerful. It was so affirming, so healing, and so creative all at once. Though I didn't realize it at the time, it was the first of many healing affirmations I would make over the next several years. Something else I didn't realize at the time was that I was about to chart my own course. I was about to come in contact with my life's purpose (well…at least one of them). I remember many times since writing my first book that I have said to other IC patients, I believe it was fate. I believe it was fate that I had such a severe case of IC and that I had so many of the other symptoms that so often come with it. I believe it was fate because I believe that I was meant to write these books and help other people to heal. But as much as I wanted to do that, help other people I mean, I also, of course, wanted to get better myself. I was desperate to get better myself. But even in that pain and desperation, I knew, somewhere inside of me I just knew, that this was not what God had intended for me. I just knew, deep down, that I would not be sick with IC for the rest of my life. In that moment, I chose to believe that I would get better. And there I was, before ever reading a thing about the mind/body/spirit connection, already using that connection in order to help me heal.

This decision not to accept the fate of "incurable" was the first of many choices that I had to make (that we all have to make) after getting diagnosed with IC. We have to decide not only what we think IC is about and how we are going to approach treating it (e.g., as a bladder disease or as a whole body disease, as an infection or as a defective bladder lining), we also have to decide whether to try medical treatments, alternative treatments, or a combination of both. We have to decide, once we choose medical and/or alternative treatments, which of those we will try and for how long. How do we know if we've given the treatments a fair shot? We have to decide. And even though the doctor can suggest various treatment options, only we can know how we feel physically when we take the pill or try the treatment. So in the end, we really must be the ones to decide.

As overwhelming as all of these decisions can be as to how we will treat our IC on a physical level, just as overwhelming and just as important is how we are going to treat it on a spiritual and emotional level. How will we deal with having IC? How will we deal with all the emotions that come up? How will we deal with the anger, the guilt, the shame, the depression, the frustration and the embarrassment of having a disease like IC? How will we handle the spiritual question that we all can't help but ask...why me? Will we choose to blame ourselves? Will we blame others? Will we blame God? Will we choose to think that we are just insanely unlucky? All of these emotions and all of these questions are actually decisions, choices that we all must make as we deal with having, and trying to heal from, IC.

We all have the choice whether to believe we can and will get well or whether we are going to believe that there is little or no chance of that happening. We all have a choice in our attitude toward having IC. Will we view it as a challenge or as a burden? Will we view it as something we have to learn to accept and live with the rest of our lives or as something to be overcome? It is up to us to decide. And please don't be mistaken. It *does* matter which we choose.

Many wise men throughout history and every master who has ever walked the planet, has taught us the same lesson. Thoughts are things. They carry energy. They are part of the tools of creation.

"As ye think, so shall ye be." - Jesus
"What we think, we become." - Buddha

"The world we have created is a product of our thinking; it cannot be changed without changing our thinking." – Albert Einstein
"Our life is what our thoughts make it." - Marcus Aurelius Antoninus

Knowing that "thoughts are things", knowing that our attitude and our perspective of something can and does affect our reality of that "thing", it is very difficult for me to watch as people out there continue every day to take hope away from IC patients. They tell the IC patient that they can *never* get better. That there is only remission, that there is no cure. They tell them that the best they can really hope for is remission. And they tell them that if anyone ever tells you that they are all better, that they are cured of IC, then they are either lying to you or they never had IC in the first place. This is how strongly they feel there is no cure. There are those who discourage stories of hope and healing and see them as something that offers the IC patient what they call "false hope". They not only assume it is "false"; they believe it is actually harmful that the IC patient have any hope at all. The IC patient is told to mourn their old self. They are told that they will "just have to learn to live with it". Hope for a medical cure, yes, but don't be so bold as to think that YOU can get your own body better. And if an IC patient speaks out and says that they are better, they are told, "Just wait, it'll come back. You only THINK you are better." Even in the midst of feeling better and being free from symptoms, that doubt and negative belief in the incurable-ness of IC, can haunt even the most positive, happy former IC patient. Causing them to wonder, are they really better? Will their IC come back? This is how strongly IC patients are convinced that there is no hope to completely heal from IC. And so it goes, under the guise of protection, those who would take all hope from the IC patient continue, without realizing or intending I'm sure, to take that vision of complete wellness away from the patient. I assume they are unaware of just how valuable that vision is.

Now of course it is true that there is no known medical cure for IC. But, as I've said in my first two books, just because "they" haven't figured it out yet, does NOT mean that you can't get better. People were getting better from cancer long before they came up with any medical cures. There have been people who have gotten themselves better from all kinds of "incurable" diseases. Incurable diseases are only called incurable because there is no known *medical* cure. It does not mean that the disease is truly incurable.

There are people with any illness, not just IC, who feel discouraged, depressed, and without hope to get well. Their attitude may be totally justified due to circumstances that they believe are out of their control. They feel they have no hope because medically there is not much that can be done. Feeling that there is no chance of getting better when you are suffering physically can make anyone feel depressed, frustrated, and discouraged. And of course it is understandable to believe the "experts" when they tell you that not much can be done. But many of us forget that we have our own inner resources. We forget about our own God given ability to help heal our own body.

Whether you choose the medical or alternative route in treating your IC, whether you choose to treat your IC as an infection or as an autoimmune disease, whether you choose to think of IC as a defect in the bladder lining or as a result of a back injury, it doesn't matter. You can STILL utilize your own inner resources, your own healing power. We all have it. Whether we choose to use it is up to us. If there is anything I've learned from having IC it's that we have the power to help heal ourselves. It is within us even when we don't feel like it is. We just have to choose to believe.

Maybe you are tired and maybe you feel like you just don't have it in you to fight your way back to health. Maybe you're reading this thinking, I've had IC for 14 years and changing my way of thinking is not going to make it go away. And you know what I would say to you? You are absolutely right. That is not *all* it will take. It is not some kind of magic trick where you can start thinking you will heal and the next day you will be all better. It doesn't work like that. We have to take action on the physical level as well. But always remember, you are still in there. You are more than *just* your body. You are also spirit, a spark of the Divine, a soul living in (and around) a physical body. So even when you are sick with IC and don't feel like yourself or look like yourself, know that you are *still* in there and that you *still* have the ability to affect your healing. Even if your body has changed because of IC, even if you can't do all the things that you used to be able to do, even if you don't feel like yourself because you're so sick of being sick all the time, you still have your mind and your spirit that can help you heal. You can still find a way back to yourself and the health you once knew.

I know that for me, healing, in many ways, was a journey back to me. And I mean that on every level. As I was healing on a physical level, so was I healing on an emotional and spiritual level even when I didn't realize it at the time. In fact, the next decision I made after getting diagnosed, after deciding that I was going to get better, had to do with my treatment choices. And though I didn't realize it back then, it was truly the start of my healing on every level.

The only urologist in the city where I live that knew of IC and was willing to treat IC patients wanted to give me bladder instillations. That was his treatment choice for me. And even though I had been diagnosed with a severe case of IC by one of his friends just six weeks before, he told me that if I wasn't willing to give his treatment choice a try then it must mean that I wasn't in that much pain. I told him about what I had learned from talking to other IC patients and how I was interested in some of the other treatment options available. I told him that invasive procedures and catheters only caused me more pain and that I wanted to try something else. He was not pleased. He refused to prescribe pain medication if I would not proceed with his treatment protocol. And though I had been suffering for over 5 weeks without any pain medication, I still chose to refuse his bladder instillations. I walked out of his office and never went back. This was the first step on my healing journey, both physically and spiritually. There I was sticking up for myself, protecting my body from what I knew *for me* would be more harm, and following what my gut instincts were telling me to do. (Well...all except for the fact that I didn't punch him in the face before walking out. Just kidding.) This decision was really the first point on my healing journey where I chose to listen to my body and myself over what someone else was telling me to do. It was therefore also the decision that marked the start of my spiritual journey back to me.

Naïve and ignorant, maybe, but I forged ahead regardless. I did not want to give the responsibility of my healing over to "the doctor" because I was well aware that in many ways they were just guessing at what they were doing. And I don't mean that as a criticism, but merely as a fact. Guessing is all that it *can* be when nothing is proven yet. It is all trial and error no matter what treatment you try, whether medical or alternative, we all know that. I decided to take my chances with myself. (Not that I recommend this for anyone else, this is just what felt right for me.) I knew I hadn't gone to medical school or anything, but I also knew that I wasn't an idiot. I could read the medical studies, study the body and my symptoms and figure this thing out myself. I mean, how hard could it be? (Like I said, naïve and ignorant.)

But you know what? It didn't even matter. It didn't matter that I was naïve and ignorant as to how complicated IC could be. And it also didn't matter that I was not what you would call a very disciplined person. I didn't heal from IC because I followed some regimented treatment plan. I didn't drink marshmallow root tea religiously 3 times a day or stick to the IC diet or anti-candida diet without cheating. I also made a lot of mistakes along the way as I've described in my other books (with the hope that you could avoid them). I certainly didn't do everything perfectly. And you know what? It didn't even matter. Charlie and I were talking about this just the other day. It was really the belief that I would get better that was the magnet pulling me forward. As long as I believed I would get better, pictured myself better, thanked God for healing me (even before I "felt" healed), I was getting better. And it wasn't magic either. I didn't get better because I was some kind of ultra lucky person and I didn't get better by only *thinking* that I would get better. I had to take action. I had to take a LOT of action. I had to make some tough changes in my life like quitting smoking, changing my eating habits, giving up certain things for a time while I was healing, and forcing myself to get back into exercising regularly even when I was still in pain. I also had to get rid of toxic relationships and stressful situations as much as possible and I absolutely had to start putting myself first for a change. None of these things were easy things for me to do. I also had to do a lot of reading and research, a lot of talking to other IC patients, and a lot of discussing things with Charlie before I could figure out what I should do next. It was definitely a combination of believing and action. But by thinking that I would get better, by believing that I would, somehow, through the special magic of God/the Universe, I was led to the answers. Somehow I muddled through, figured things out, and healed physically.

Knowing that where thoughts go, energy flows, I focused my thoughts on healing. We speak to ourselves inside our heads all the time. I knew that my thoughts in every moment were helping to create my life. And I knew that I had a choice about what I was going to think about during all those moments. I knew it was just as easy to think a positive thought, as it was to think a negative one. I knew that thinking negatively was only going to make me feel worse in the moment anyway. And now of course I realize that thinking negatively in the moment was only going to create more negativity in my future moments. What goes around comes around. What we put out, is reflected right back to us. This is not only true of our actions, but of our thoughts as well.

I searched for answers in every area of my body (since I had symptoms in every area) and on every level (physical, emotional, and spiritual). I went to the library and signed out dozens of medical books and later on, dozens of herb and alternative medicine books. I searched the Internet and spoke to IC patients constantly. When doctors didn't have answers for what was happening inside my body, I went to medical intuitives to see what they had to say. And though they were not always accurate, they did provide me with insights into the connections between my symptoms and my spirit, my symptoms and my thoughts, my symptoms and my feelings. They were the catalyst, along with the books I was reading at the time, for me to learn more about the mind/body/spirit connection.

One of the first things I learned after reading about the mind/body/spirit connection was that it is not just about discovering what spiritual and emotional issues may have led up to our getting sick, it was also about using that connection in order to get better. The mind/body/spirit connection is not about blame. It's about power. It's about the God given power we have inside ourselves to affect our own healing. After all, if our mind and spirit are that powerful that they can lead us (without us even realizing it) to getting sick in the first place, they can surely help lead us back to health.

"The natural healing force within each one of us is the greatest force in getting well."
- Hippocrates

Chapter 5

The Mysteries of IC

It felt as if I got blindsided. Yet really, the signs were there all the time. I just wasn't paying any attention. I was so wrapped up in everyday life and just trying to get through it that I wasn't noticing the symptoms I was experiencing. I didn't even think I HAD any symptoms. I wasn't noticing any of the messages I was getting from my body, from the universe, or from my own gut feelings. And when I did notice them, I ended up ignoring them anyway. And then one day, I woke up with IC and I thought, what the hell happened?! How did I get here?

At first when I looked at IC, all I saw was mystery. Nothing seemed to make sense about why I had it, what had caused it, or how I was going to get rid of it. Yet now, as I described in *Along the Healing Path*, looking back, I can see just how I developed IC on a physical level. On a physical level, now that I know the different causal factors involved, now that I know what I know about IC, I can see how I was all set up to get it by the time I had the surgery that initially appeared to have caused it. I can see now that all the signs were there. Now that I know what all was involved in my getting better, it's so much easier to see what all was involved in my getting sick to begin with. It's always easier to understand something when you're looking back on it. It's while we are in the midst of it, while we are living through it, that it feels so confusing, overwhelming and mysterious.

When I was first diagnosed, I was definitely confused and overwhelmed. There I was with dozens of symptoms and all they could find wrong with me was that I had some strange bladder disease that I had never even heard of! What about all the other symptoms? Why did I have them and what was I supposed to do about them? Hell, what was I supposed to do about the bladder symptoms?! It's not like there were many answers provided me by the doctors I saw. They had very little to say about the IC and even less to say about the other symptoms. I will always be grateful to my father-in-law who provided me with a computer at the very moment in my life that I needed it most. (One of many miracles that became part of my healing.) I believe it arrived just a few short weeks before I was diagnosed. Thank God I was diagnosed in the age of the Internet. I immediately got on line and found other IC patients to talk to. I learned what we all learn shortly after being diagnosed. We are all different. None of us has the same symptoms, none of us are helped by the same treatments, there is no known cause, and there is no medical cure. I learned right away that there were to be no easy answers when it came to IC. Learning to understand IC was, for me, a process that would take several years.

Like many IC patients with more moderate to severe cases, I had many other symptoms besides bladder symptoms. Please know that you're not alone if you have some of these other symptoms (many of us do) and also know that just because you have IC does not mean you will necessarily acquire all of these other symptoms. As I said, one of the first things we realize with IC is that we are all different in what symptoms we experience and also in what helps us with those symptoms. With my IC came fairly severe symptoms of fibromyalgia (muscle and joint pain) and IBS (irritable bowel syndrome), as well as vulvodynia, systemic candida (yeast), multiple chemical sensitivities and food allergies, hypothyroidism, kidney stones and kidney infections, swollen glands all over my body, major problems with my teeth and gums, nausea and acid stomach, dry hair, skin, eyes, and mouth, bloating in the pelvic area, edema (swelling all over), hip pain, night sweats and also lack of "normal" perspiration during the day, pain at the base of my neck, cold hands and feet with an inability to tolerate extreme temperatures (Charlie used to say that I had a broken thermostat) and lower back pain. Along with the bleeding ulcers in my bladder, of course, came symptoms of severe pain, constant urgency and frequency that was so out of control that you could safely say that I lived in the bathroom. To be even more specific I also had difficulty initiating the stream (in other words, nothing would come out no matter how hard I tried), pain that increased as my bladder filled and also pain that increased immediately following urination due to bladder spasms. I had burning pain within my bladder and also during urination, sharp shooting pains up the urethra into my bladder (they felt like they shot right up the middle of me), the mysterious bubbles in the urine that IC patients sometimes notice, the cloudy looking urine, the pieces of tissue with blood attached in the urine, and the never knowing if I had a "regular bladder infection" or if it was "just" IC. When my IC was still severe and even as I was getting better initially, I felt as if I were full of poison, as if there were acids burning in my system. I also felt full of infection with the swollen glands, low-grade fevers, earaches, sore throats and flu-like symptoms. This, all of this, is what IC felt like to me.

Because I suffered such a dramatic onset to my IC, it was much easier for me to see that all of my other symptoms were connected. It's not as easy to tell when you develop all these other symptoms and illnesses over time. The fact that all the different symptoms are all called by different names, diagnosed by different medical specialists, and treated as completely different diseases (or problems), doesn't help either. But many of us have these other symptoms and illnesses with our IC and I felt there had to be a reason. My first understanding of IC was, and is still something I very much believe to this day, that IC is NOT just a bladder disease.

I still believe that physically, I would not have been able to get better had I not treated my whole body together as a unit, instead of just treating my bladder. If I would have treated my bladder with little regard to these other symptoms and then treated my other symptoms with little regard to my bladder, as if they were not connected, as if they were separate problems, I know for certain that I would not have been able to get better. Maybe I would have been able to get into temporary remissions, but without getting to the root of the problem and addressing my whole body, I know it would not have been possible for me to heal from IC. This is the reason I so strongly believe that we must strive, both individually and research-wise, to understand the IC body, not just the IC bladder.

Understanding IC is not only a challenge to the medical community, but to each one of us. Each person with IC must determine what he or she believes IC is all about. With no proven cause, we are left to choose which theory we agree with. Because we are all different in our symptoms and in how we acquired IC, we all have to determine what IC is FOR US. If you believe that IC is a bladder disease and that treating your bladder symptoms with medications and instillations is the way to heal it, then that is the way to go for you. If you believe that your IC is caused by diet or food allergies, then watching what you eat is obviously a good way to approach your healing. If you believe that your IC is hormone related or an autoimmune disease, you will obviously treat it differently than if you believe your IC was caused by a back injury/problem or by bacteria. If you believe, as I do, that IC is more than just a bladder disease; if you have multiple other symptoms that you believe are related to your IC, then treating your whole body together (i.e., taking a holistic approach), rather than treating just your bladder is the way to go for you. As I said, we all have to make these types of decisions with IC because nothing is clear cut or proven. Until "they" discover a scientifically proven cause and/or cure for IC, we are truly on our own in determining what we believe is causing and perpetuating our IC symptoms.

Just because taking a natural, holistic approach to treating my IC was right for me, doesn't mean it will be right for you. As you may already know, I am a big believer in each of us doing what we feel most comfortable with. I feel that especially with a disease like IC where we are all so different, it is important to make treatment decisions based on our own individual IC situation. Only we can decide what we feel comfortable doing (and allowing others to do) to *our* body. I have also always stressed the importance of listening to our own gut instincts after learning as much as we possibly can about the treatment(s) first, by not only talking to the doctor, but to other IC patients as well. Listening to the experiences of other IC patients firsthand is so very important. Other IC patients will offer you much greater insight into the treatments than the doctors can just because they are the ones who have actually experienced them. They are the ones who live with the repercussions of those treatments, whether good or bad. In fact, in trying to understand the IC body, my best source of information was other IC patients. I spent countless hours on the phone and on line speaking with them. I watched for the differences among us and was especially searching for the commonalities. It was often in those commonalities that I would find answers.

Yes, we definitely have differences among us, but we do also have some things in common. Those commonalities are what I focused on initially in order to understand my IC body. One of our major commonalities that I discussed in much greater length in my first two books is the toxic body. It is my opinion that most IC patients, especially those with more severe cases, often have a toxic body. Signs of toxicity, symptoms that are classic of someone with a toxic colon and toxic body, are commonly found in IC patients. One of those classic symptoms of toxicity and another common thread between us is having multiple allergies. Of course it depends on the severity of someone's IC, but the vast majority of IC patients have allergies and sensitivities to various medications, foods, and things in the environment. Many of us become very sensitive, not only to things we ingest and are exposed to in the environment, but also to things like invasive treatments that might not bother a "normal" healthy person, to the dye used in certain medical tests like IVP's or catscans, and to the Novocain used at the dentist. IC patients are known to be sensitive not only to synthetic, chemical, and toxic things, but also to natural things, things that are normally considered to be "good for us". This is a sign that the body and the colon are toxic. Speaking of which, another common symptom among IC patients is to have intestinal problems.

Many IC patients are diagnosed with or have symptoms of IBS (irritable bowel syndrome), but there are also many other intestinal disorders (whether polyps, diverticulitis, chronic constipation, or whatever) that can also be found among IC patients.

Another thing we have in common is the fact that most of us have multiple symptoms aside from bladder symptoms. And not only do we have multiple symptoms; we also have multiple *causes* for some of those symptoms. This, in my opinion, has made IC even more confusing to the doctors and researchers. Because IC is many things, because it is different for each person, because there are different factors involved in "the cause" for each person AND because for each person's there may even be multiple causes for each particular symptom, it is not likely that they will find "THE" cause of IC. I don't believe there is going to be a "the cause" of IC, but rather, "here are the possible causes of your individual case of IC". From there, there will have to be work done on an individual basis to determine the cause(s) for that person for ALL of their IC and IC related symptoms. That is why understanding the IC body takes more than just reading everything you can about IC. It takes more than talking with your doctor about treatment options and more than going to support group meetings and talking to other IC patients. Even though all four of those things are very important and helpful things to do, understanding the IC body takes even more than that. Understanding really begins after you do those four things. It really begins with YOUR body and YOUR symptoms.

Now I can't tell you exactly what caused your IC because we are all different, but I can tell you what caused mine. And I do believe, because I had such a severe case and also because of what I have seen in thousands of other IC patients, that many of the factors that were involved in my IC are fairly common causal factors in other people's IC as well. Not everyone will have as many causal factors as I did, but some of them might be and maybe even just one of them might be the same.

As I said, understanding what caused my IC was a process, and often, as I addressed one symptom, another would get worse or a new one would pop up. For example, initially I thought infection was the cause of my IC. After all, I had woken up from surgery for a ruptured ovarian cyst with symptoms of a horrible bladder and kidney infection. I was given IV antibiotics and then sent home with a prescription. It was my first bladder infection and the bladder symptoms never really went away. More antibiotics, actually, stronger antibiotics were given to me to eradicate whatever was left of that lingering infection. It was either Bactrim or Flagyl, I can't remember which, but this was when I developed my first fibromyalgia symptoms. I assumed I was allergic to the stronger antibiotic, and that's why I had developed this horrible joint pain. (Well, I didn't just assume I was allergic, that was what my doctor told me.) And even though before this surgery I never had any allergies to any medications, I accepted that explanation. However, the joint pain did not go away after I stopped taking the antibiotics. And still I had bladder symptoms. And still I thought my IC was bacteria related. I had other reasons to believe it was bacteria. I had other symptoms of infection, such as low-grade fevers every day and swollen glands all over my body, especially at the top of my legs right near my bladder, which at times hurt so much that it was very difficult to walk. And of course I had symptoms similar to a bladder infection (e.g., bleeding, pain, burning, constant urgency, and frequency). So before I got into a more natural approach to healing, I tried long term antibiotic therapy. And even though this is a "medical" type of therapy because it uses synthetic, pharmaceutical medications, it was still considered "alternative" because it is not the typical mainstream medical way to treat IC. In fact, medically, for the most part, they don't consider IC to be bacteria related. As far as I know, no one has been able to explain yet why there are some IC patients who are helped by antibiotics.

Even though bacteria were definitely involved in my IC, long-term antibiotics were not enough to get me better. They were not THE answer for me. However, they did provide me some much needed relief, they did stop the majority of the bleeding from my bladder and therefore took the pain down a considerable notch, and they did lead me to my next causal factor, which was yeast. I had developed a horrible systemic candida (yeast) problem from taking so many antibiotics. I later learned that yeast might have been a causal factor even before I got on the long-term antibiotic therapy, but I just hadn't realized it. And even though systemic candida was definitely a factor in my IC, cleansing the yeast was still not enough to get me better. At this point I was learning much more about the toxic body from reading all about candida and a toxic colon. I started to realize that I had a lot of the classic symptoms of a toxic body. I also began to realize that as I was cleansing my colon and body of yeast and other toxins, I was still smoking (i.e., inhaling toxins/poisons) and putting other chemicals into my body with pharmaceutical medications, the foods I was eating, and the things I was exposing myself to in the environment. I knew, in order for me to give my body the chance to heal, that all had to stop.

As much as I didn't want to at the time, I knew I had to quit smoking. I knew it was adding more chemicals and poisons into my body. Even though smoking was a factor in my IC (or at least part of my inability to heal from IC), quitting smoking was not enough to get me better. In fact, right after I quit, I got even worse. I learned that horrible lesson that I have already shared with you in my first two books. Whenever you remove a source of toxicity to your body, your body will react and begin to cleanse itself. And in the process, we can experience even worse symptoms than we had to begin with. This is because, for a time, we become even more toxic than we were when the source was still present. First I had yeast die-off reactions from cleansing the yeast and then I had horrible edema along with extreme chemical sensitivities and allergies to just about everything from quitting smoking. I had already realized that I had developed allergies to various medications (e.g., antibiotics, pain medications, antihistamines) since getting IC, but things got much more out of control after I quit smoking. I couldn't be around anything that was toxic. Not perfume, cigarette smoke, exhaust fumes, gasoline fumes, chemical cleaners, and even fumes from the dishwasher made me sick. (Before that point in my life I never even knew that there were fumes that came out of a dishwasher!) Anyway, it was at this point in my healing that I discovered NAET (an allergy elimination technique using acupressure and/or acupuncture and kinesiology which I also discussed in my first two books) to get rid of all these allergies. Again my symptoms changed. Some got worse before they started getting better, while others improved right away. As the allergies were being eliminated, it was easy to see that my newfound allergies were affecting nearly all of my symptoms. And though allergies were definitely a factor in my IC and IC related symptoms, getting rid of the allergies still wasn't enough to get me all better.

Another thing that got horrible after I quit smoking was my teeth and gums. All of a sudden I got blisters in my throat and mouth, sore and swollen gums (some of which began receding), my teeth were moving around in my mouth from the swollen gums and they were actually chipping for no apparent reason. This was occurring right before and during the allergy elimination treatments and led me to another causal factor in my IC, yet another source of toxicity to my body that had to be removed, my dental fillings. To make a long story short, I discovered that the metal in my fillings were a source of poison that my body simply could not handle. I knew I had to replace all of my mercury amalgam fillings to help me get better. (This was the case for me. It will not necessarily be the case for everyone.) And even though the poison from my fillings was definitely a huge factor in my IC, having my fillings replaced *still* was not enough to get me all the way better. I still had more work to do.

After having the last of my mercury fillings replaced as my first book was published, some of my IC and IC related symptoms improved immediately, others changed more slowly, and still others got temporarily worse. Many people ask me about this so I wanted to make sure to let you know. By the time *To Wake In Tears* was published and I wrote the first chapter to this book, my bladder symptoms were pretty much non-existent, but my IBS definitely got worse for a while after the mercury was removed from my teeth. Of course, the poison had to get out of my body somehow and it sure was. My sinuses went completely nuts at first. They went from bad to worse as all the poison drained from my head. My ears even seemed to drain. My glands slowly went down and my fibromyalgia symptoms definitely improved. At that point, a couple years ago, I still had some joint pain when the weather got bad (though not near as bad as it had been) and I still had some muscle weakness from the pressure of the edema (which was also not near as bad as it had been). I was still having cleansing reactions (healing crisis) especially around my period (which of course is a natural cleanse) and especially if I took or did something additional to help me cleanse (which of course I was still doing for about another year after having my fillings replaced). The pain at the base of my neck was getting a lot better and my thyroid didn't hurt as much if something pressed on it (like a turtleneck or something). My earaches were getting better and so were my sore throats though the blisters are still there today as I write this. They still haven't healed all the way yet. The only bladder symptom I had left at that point was that the vibrating in the car still bothered me by causing urgency. I believed at the time that this symptom would go away when the rest of the pelvic area swelling went down. I felt it was due to the pressure on my bladder that this was still happening because it was always worse during the second half of my cycle when I was the most swollen in the pelvic area. My frequency was WAY down even two years ago. Where I used to go 80-100 times a day when my IC was severe and my bladder was bleeding, two years ago I was going about 10-15 times a day depending on how much water I drank. (A seriously huge improvement.) I no longer had any bleeding from my bladder or infections in my bladder or kidneys. For the past few years I have had no kidney stones, kidney pain, bladder pain, or pain while urinating. For the past couple years I have been able to eat and drink whatever I want without it causing any bladder symptoms. All the allergies I had cleared with NAET are still gone (it's been well over two years since my last NAET treatment), but it doesn't mean that I'm not still nervous at times to try new things. Two years ago I still had sensitivity in a couple of the teeth where I had fillings replaced. It took some time for that to get better, maybe a year or so, but now they are fine. As the months passed, I was healing and getting stronger in every way. Once I had my fillings replaced (of course I had already removed all the other sources of toxicity to my body that I was aware of), I never went backwards in my healing again. Well...all except for the anxiety problem I've been telling you about.

Actually, by the time I sat back down to finish writing this book, I had three remaining symptoms from my IC. I couldn't consider myself 100 percent back to normal until these symptoms were resolved. Whenever anyone would ask me if I was cured of IC, I always told them that I was still healing. And of course, I was, and still am, healing as I write this book. I am still dealing with the anxiety problem that I wrote about in the first two chapters. I still have some edema and my skin is still messed up. Not that my skin is a serious symptom, but still. I had been blessed with wonderful skin all of my life, but since getting IC, my skin became a mess. It was breaking out on my arms, legs, chest, and nearly every part of my body! At first I thought it was from all the cleansing because my skin definitely got worse when I began cleansing, but it still hadn't gotten better so I knew there was definitely something else going on. I had used all kinds of great skin care products and none of it made any difference at all, which of course confirmed what I already knew was the case, that it was being caused from something inside of me.

As annoyed and frustrated as I felt with these remaining symptoms, I knew I needed to stay positive. I knew I needed to address the remainder of my symptoms the same way that I had addressed all of my other IC symptoms. I needed to look at them from every perspective possible. Not only individually and collectively, but also physically, emotionally, and spiritually. I needed to do a lot of research and discover what all my options were first. And most importantly, I needed to listen to my body.

"The body, like everything else in life, is a mirror of our inner thoughts and beliefs. The body is always talking to us, if we will only take time to listen. Every cell within your body responds to every single thought you think and every word you speak."
-   Louise L. Hay (*You Can Heal Your Life*)

Chapter 6

---◆---

Listening to the IC Body

Just as understanding my IC was a process, so was learning to listen to my body. When I first got sick and my IC was still severe, it was very difficult to listen to my body. At that time I was still so toxic and full of infection that all I felt was miserable. I was always in so much pain and feeling so incredibly uncomfortable with the urgency, so thoroughly exhausted from the frequency, and so completely stressed out trying to deal with what to do about all of it, that it was very difficult to "hear" anything. It was hard to distinguish between all my symptoms (e.g., how much was bladder pain, how much was pelvic pain, was it a "regular" bladder infection or was it the IC). In the beginning it was definitely harder to know what was causing what or what was making me feel worse. It got easier for me to notice the connections and what was causing my symptoms to increase as I became less toxic and less infected. As time went on I learned to pay very close attention to how I was feeling. By writing down my symptoms and then keeping track of what I ate, what I was exposed to, what was going on in my life in terms of stress, or if it was during my menstrual cycle or whatever, I began to understand more of what was affecting me on a physical level. And as I became less toxic I was also able to *feel* more and therefore distinguish more between my symptoms. But don't get me wrong, it still wasn't easy.

Listening to the IC body is NOT easy. Trying to understand our symptoms in terms of what is causing them and what is making them worse can be a daily (even hourly for some people) endeavor. But

61

finding some understanding of our symptoms can help us determine what to do about them. For example, maybe we realize that whenever we eat or drink certain things, our bladder hurts more or whenever we stand or sit for too long, our bladder starts to spasm, or whenever we are exposed to perfume or paint fumes our bladder hurts more, etc. We can avoid the basic IC no-no's in terms of food, for example, but because we are all different, we each have to figure out what WE can tolerate eating. The only way to do that is to listen to our body. Because we are all different and because the doctors can't tell us what is causing our symptoms, we are left to figure it out for ourselves. The best way for us to do that is to listen to our body because *our* body is not going to be exactly like another IC patient's body.

There are several ways to listen to your body on a physical level. The obvious ways are when you feel tired, you rest...when you are hungry, you eat...when you have to go to the bathroom, you go. These are basic ways "normal" people listen to their body every day. Or do they? Some of us don't rest when we are tired, we don't always eat when we are hungry (of course some of us eat even when we're not hungry) and we don't always go to the bathroom when we have to go (maybe we have IC and are doing bladder holding protocol, maybe we are busy at work and not able to go when we need to, etc.) Some people are so busy with the "stuff" of life that they ignore even the most basic needs of their body. I know that before I ever got sick with IC, I really wasn't listening to my body at all. I'm not proud to tell you that more often than not I was ignoring my body's needs. I was not overly concerned about what I was putting into my body in terms of food or drink (plus I was smoking cigarettes). I had stopped exercising shortly after college and often I didn't rest when I should have. I was under a lot of stress and I wasn't giving my body what it needed in order to handle that stress. I wasn't getting enough rest and I wasn't getting enough nutrition from the types of foods I was eating. I was definitely not paying attention to what my body was trying to tell me. Heck, back then I didn't even know it was "talking" to me. I was relatively young and basically a healthy person, so the fact that I was ignoring my body's needs was not something I was even concerned about. I guess I just figured that I could handle it. But it's like with stress, sometimes you don't realize how much it is affecting you.

Listening to your body means giving it what it needs and not doing things that hurt it. While I was getting better from IC I learned that listening to my body meant not only paying attention to what it needed and what it was asking for, it also meant acting on that information. That was definitely the harder part for me. I know many of us with IC who ignore the needs of our body in order to please other people (and even sometimes to please ourselves). I know I used to do it. Sometimes we do things like make dinner, clean the house, have sex with our spouse, or go out somewhere, etc. even when we know it's going to make us feel worse. Some of us feel as if we have no choice. I mean, who is going to make dinner then? Who is going to clean the house if we don't do it? And who is going to have sex with our spouse if we don't? Seriously. Will they start to look elsewhere? I know this is a very real concern for many IC patients. I know so many IC patients who have sex with their spouse even though it's painful for them and they might have to pay the price for days afterward. Many of us go places and do things because we feel guilty not to go or do them (we feel bad saying "no") or maybe because sometimes we really *want* to go (even though we know there is a pretty good chance it will make us feel worse). I also know many IC patients who ignore what their body is telling them when they take a medication for example. The doctor tells them to take the medication, their family thinks they should listen to the doctor, *they* think they should listen to the doctor, and to stop taking the medication just because their body is not reacting well to it, to them, it just seems like the wrong thing to do. Listening to other people over what our body is telling us (based on how it's feeling), listening to other people over what our own gut instincts are telling us, and listening to other people because we feel like they should know what they are talking about, are mistakes that many of us make. Maybe I shouldn't call them "mistakes". For me, they were mistakes. When it came to my IC, I was *always* better off listening to my body and myself over what other people were telling me to do.

You can also take "listening to the IC body" further on a physical level. You can do things like look at your tongue and see if it looks pink, as it should, or if it has a yellowish, greenish, or white coating. Because your tongue is part of your digestive system, it will show you if something is not right inside. You can tell if you have yeast overgrowth if you have a white coating on your tongue (thrush) or if your tongue is a greenish or yellowish color it is more likely that you have a toxic colon. You can rub your feet while looking at a reflexology chart and notice all the sensitive spots. Then you can check which organ in your body that those spots correspond with. You can also use acupressure as a tool to listen to your body. Similar to reflexology, you can press on acupressure points on your body that correspond with various organs within your body. This way you can identify where you have blockages and weaknesses. And of course you can also use these tools to help release blockages and strengthen weaknesses. They do all of this and more in Chinese medicine where they can also (believe it or not) listen to the tone of your voice and are then able to tell things about your health. There is a specialty called Iridology where they can look at your eyes and are then able to tell what is going on in your body. Something like NAET is also a form of listening to your body. NAET is used to identify what the body is sensitive/allergic to and in that way it is a form of listening to the body. Really any healing method using kinesiology or muscle testing (as NAET does) is a form of listening to the body. There are so many ways to listen to your body. And with IC, utilizing as many as possible can be extremely helpful because there is so much mystery with our symptoms and there are so many connections to be made. With IC, there is so much to understand.

It is important to listen to our body so that we can understand our symptoms, not only on a physical level, but on an emotional and spiritual level as well. We are living in a world where there isn't time for doctors to look at or try to understand the spiritual and emotional aspects of illness. We have to look to our own spiritual and emotional issues as to why we got sick. What is our body trying to tell us? What is our illness trying to tell us? By looking at the symbolic meaning of our symptoms and reflecting on our feelings, we can gain a deeper insight into why we are sick and why we have the specific symptoms we do. We can choose to look at our lives as well as our bodies to notice where we are leaking energy, where we have blockages, how we are living (or had lived) that was not in accordance with the desires of our soul. Maybe it is a job, maybe it is a relationship, maybe it is several relationships, or maybe we are not being true to ourselves for whatever the reason(s). All of these things can influence our health. And I know for me, all of them did.

Just like physically, looking back, I can now more easily see how and why I got IC on a more emotional/spiritual level as well. But I have to tell you; it certainly wasn't obvious to me for quite some time. It wasn't like I started reading about the mind/body/spirit "stuff" and immediately understood why I got sick. But looking back on my life as I looked at the symbolic meaning of my various symptoms, eventually I did start to unravel the mystery. It's not easy to admit these things to you because some of the issues are embarrassing for me to talk about, but I feel it's important to share them with you because I think some of the things that were involved in my getting IC on an emotional and spiritual level might be things that have led other people to IC as well. Just as we have things in common physically, so we will have things in common spiritually and emotionally. And of course, on the flip side, just as we are all different physically, we will not all be exactly the same in terms of the spiritual and emotional issues involved in our IC.

There are those who believe that everything that passes through our perception has a message for us about ourselves. They believe that every part of our life is an expression of our inner self. Our family, our car, our job, our spouse, our pets, our home, and of course, even our illness, can be seen as a reflection of our inner self. Some people believe that our body has a consciousness, that it is like a sponge, absorbing everything...absorbing what we feed it both in our thoughts and in our spoken words, in what we eat or don't eat, in our action or inaction, in what we expose it to and in what we put into it. Our bodies are reflecting back to us what we are feeding them, physically, emotionally, and spiritually. You've heard the phrases "You are what you eat." "You are what you think." "What you put in, comes out." Listening to our body is a way to see what we have been feeding it.

As I was saying, every symptom we experience in whatever illness we have, has a message for us about ourselves. Our body, according to some, tells our higher self (or our soul) a story about our mental and emotional make-up. Our body is not only a vessel and a temple for our spirit; it is also a messenger for our soul on the physical plane. It holds onto all of our fears, hopes and joys. It holds onto all the ideas and beliefs that we hold about reality. Being sick, I learned, is a time to go within, a special time to tune into the messages that our bodies are sending us.

This was to become a whole new way for me to listen to my body. But I have to be honest; at first I wasn't at all sure if I bought into the whole symbolic meaning of each body part thing. At first when I would read about a symptom I would think, *that* isn't me, that symbolic message doesn't apply to *me*. But then one day I decided to write them all down in a list and I couldn't help but notice that there were certain themes running through them. I'll show you what I mean. Here was my list. I'm copying it from a crinkled up piece of paper from nearly five years ago. I saved it by sticking it into one of my favorite symbolism books by Louise Hay called *Heal your Body*. I used that book, along with another favorite of mine by Denise Linn called *The Secret Language of Signs*, to come up with the following list of the possible symbolic meanings of all of my IC related symptoms.

IC Symbols

Symptom | Possible symbolic message
Bladder problems | Being "pissed off" – Anger
 | Anxiety
 | Holding on to old ideas or beliefs
 | Fear of letting go

66

Symptom	Possible symbolic message
Inflammation	Seeing red, inflamed thinking – Anger Frustration
Urinary Infections (and Urethritis)	Being "pissed off" – Anger Blame
Ulcers	Fear A belief that you're not good enough Something is eating away at you
Bleeding	Joy running out The draining away of energy or life
force	Anger
Diseases ending in "itis"	Anger and frustration regarding conditions in your life
Pain	Guilt
Spasms	Tightening our thoughts through fear

IBS Symbols

Symptom	Possible symbolic message
Bowel problems	Fear of letting go of the old and no longer needed Intestines have to do with the ease of elimination
Diarrhea	Fear
Constipation	Refusing to release old ideas, stuck in the past

Symptom	Possible symbolic message
Spasms	Tightening our thoughts through fear

Fibromyalgia Symbols

Symptom	Possible symbolic message
Muscles	Represent our ability to move in life
Joints	Represent changes in direction in life and the ease of those movements
Edema/swelling	Holding onto something

(Each area of the body affected has a different meaning.)

Knees	Represent pride and ego Fear Inflexibility
Ankles	Represent our mobility in life Inflexibility Guilt
Hands	Express our state of being (e.g., close fisted or open handed)
Shoulders	Shouldering responsibility or carrying burdens
Neck	Inflexibility
Arms	Represent how you embrace experiences in life
Legs	Represent your foundation, what carries you forward in life

Other IC Related Symbols

Symptom	Possible symbolic message
Cramps	Tension Fear Gripping or holding on
Cysts	A false growth Running the old painful movies Nursing hurts
Ear aches (or ear problems)	Anger Not wanting to hear
Hypothyroidism	Giving up Feeling hopelessly stifled
Jaw problems	Anger Resentment
Kidney problems	Criticism Disappointment Shame Fear
Kidney Stones	Lumps of anger not dissolved
Vulvodynia	Feeling vulnerable
Yeast Infection	Denying your own needs Not supporting yourself
Thrush (yeast in mouth, white coated tongue)	Anger over making wrong decisions

As I reviewed the symbolic meaning of all of my symptoms, I couldn't help but notice the theme of anger. Geez...there it was again! Someone else (well I guess it was a book) that was telling me I was angry. But I didn't *feel* like I was angry. And I certainly didn't *act* like I was angry. Then I thought, even if I was angry, what was I supposed to do about it? And how could I do something about it if I had no idea what I was even angry about? What I really didn't understand was... How could I be *that* angry (enough to get a severe case of IC) and not even realize it? This just didn't make any sense to me. So I put it all aside for a while. I didn't really go back to trying to understand the symbolic meaning of my symptoms or reading more about the mind/body/spirit "stuff" until after I learned more about the universal laws and about my own spirituality.

"There are only two ways to live your life.
One is as though nothing is a miracle. The other is as
though everything is a miracle."
- Albert Einstein

Chapter 7

Miracles and Messages

It had been quite a while (since college in fact) that I gave much thought to my spiritual growth or to anything spiritual really. I had gotten caught up in a hectic life of work, friends and various activities. I was wrapped up in the regular stresses of everyday life and I stopped even thinking about my soul and my "real" purpose in life. I stopped thinking about the "whys" and was just always busy doing. And then I got IC. Seemingly out of the blue I got horribly sick and now, all of a sudden I was searching for answers. I was searching for the meaning of all this.

We all have to make sense of our lives and what happens in our lives to our own satisfaction. When I was examining the question "why me?" when it came to my IC, I felt sure that there was a deeper meaning than "it just happened". Anything that is so big, that changes your life as much as IC changes your life, I felt there just *had* to be a reason. It's funny, when I was first diagnosed, even the doctors told me "it just happened". They told me this of course because they truly had no explanation for why I got IC. But just because they didn't understand why I got it, didn't mean that there wasn't a reason. In fact, as it turned out, physically, there were several reasons I got IC. And just because initially I didn't understand "why me?" on a more spiritual level, didn't mean there weren't reasons.

I used to believe that there were some things that happened by accident. That there were such things as "coincidences" and that life

73

was not solely up to us because some things "just happened". I guess I used to think that God allowed some things and not others. And though I never could imagine how He could have made those decisions, I guess I believed that it was not up to me to understand that. If I think back now I can remember that I believed that some people were just luckier than others. You know, some were blessed and others, well…not so much. I did believe in fate, but I also thought that some things were completely out of our control. I had a certain understanding of the way life works and a certain perspective of what God was all about. I gained this understanding and perspective as we all do, through parents, religion, education, and experience. I grew up in a fairly typical middle class suburban neighborhood and was raised within the Catholic religion. I had the opportunity for an excellent education and was fortunate to have parents that I could discuss things with. Still there were many things that I didn't understand, many contradictions that I never found any answers to. Yet it didn't really bother me all that much until some really bad things started happening in my otherwise "normal" life.

It's interesting how when something bad happens, we start looking to God for the reasons. How rarely (if ever) do we turn to Him and ask "why?" when something good happens? But when something bad happens, it's a whole other story. Some of us blame God or see the "bad thing" as a test or a punishment from Him. At the least, we are upset that He allowed it to happen. And we wonder why, if God can do anything, if He loves us SO much, why doesn't He help us? Why doesn't He heal us?

If there's one thing I've learned from all this, it's that when you start looking for answers, you'll find them. You'll start to see them all around you and most importantly, inside you. As you ask, it is answered. One of the secrets of the universe is that there is no such thing as time. Everything, according to physics, is happening in the exact same moment of NOW. Everything that has happened, everything that is happening, and everything that ever will happen is all happening in the eternal moment of NOW. That is a huge concept to grasp as we live in our three dimensional reality. It is difficult to live in the awareness of that fact, but if we realize it even from time to time, just enough to know and understand what it means when God said, "before you have asked, I have answered", we can realize one of the great powers of prayer, one of the great gifts of faith. When you pray, when you ask a question of God/the Universe, all you have to do is be still and listen. Wait and watch. Hear the next person you speak with, the next thing you see on television, the next thing you happen across on the Internet or the next thing you read in a book. God/the Universe speaks to us everyday through the world around us AND from within us. We can hear and *feel* the answers when we sit in silence. This is one of the main ways that God and our higher self speak to us. It is unlikely we will hear a booming voice coming down from the heavens when we ask a question in prayer. It is more likely that we will hear a whisper, a voice that sounds strangely enough, like our own, from inside our own head. We can also receive messages through our relationships, through our body, and through the symbols in our lives. Though I have to say, interpreting those messages can sometimes be quite a challenge. Sometimes we aren't able to understand a message until some time has passed. And it definitely takes practice just in paying attention to the symbols and noticing the "coincidences". If there was one thing that IC afforded me, it was the time to try and understand what God/the Universe was trying to tell me.

It was within a favorite childhood past time that I discovered many of my answers. Reading was something I had always enjoyed, but somewhere along the line I seemed to stop having the time to read anymore. Time to read was a wonderful gift I received from my IC. I read a lot while I was sick. When you are bedridden and/or spend most of your time in the bathroom, there's not too much else you can do. Certain books I was reading had a huge effect on me. I had always been interested in the metaphysical and the spiritual and with what was going in my life; I decided to go back to that. I read all of the *Conversations with God* books (by Neale Donald Walsch) as soon as they were published, not just once, but several times. I would read them myself first and then I would read them out loud to Charlie and we would talk about the different concepts in relation to our own lives. And then I would read them again partly for comfort, but also to gain greater understanding. There was so much in those books that rang true to me. So many contradictions about God and about "the way things work" in life, so many things I had trouble understanding as I was growing up, started to become much more clear to me as I read about the universal laws and the physics of the universe. I also read several books by Deepak Chopra (who is fabulous at explaining quantum physics) and Sanaya Roman's books "Personal Power through Awareness" and "Spiritual Growth: Being Your Higher Self" several times as well. The wisdom in these books brought me a new perspective, a new understanding of life, and a new understanding of God.

I began to understand that there are certain laws of nature that are at work in our lives whether we are aware of it or not. Understanding that we are made of the same energy as everything else in the universe and that there are certain physical laws of nature that apply to energy, I began to understand more how we affect our lives and our bodies with our thoughts, words, beliefs, and actions. I began looking at things more from a perspective of energy and taking into account these laws of nature or "universal laws". It's not that I hadn't heard of the universal laws before, because I had. It's just that I didn't understand the magnitude with which they were at work in my own life. I had heard of universal laws such as the law of karma, the law of attraction, and the law of cause and effect throughout my life in sayings such as "what goes around comes around", " like attracts like", "for every action, there is an equal and opposite reaction", etc. Reading about and discussing these principles, which are both scientific and spiritual all at the same time, offered me a new way to look at my life and what IC was doing in it.

Once I started looking at my life this way I could see that I had created or "drawn to me" pretty much every situation I have ever found myself in. By the choices I made, by what I believed to be true, by the way I acted (or didn't act) and the way I felt, by what I thought and what I said, I had been creating the circumstances of my life whether I was paying attention to it or not. At first, this was not easy for me to face. I didn't want to believe that I had that much responsibility for what had happened in my life. It was much more comfortable for me to blame other people for what they "did to me", to blame circumstances or "coincidences", or even to blame God or fate, for the things that went wrong in my life. But once I started to see my part in what had gone on in my life and in my relationships (the good and the bad), I had to start admitting to myself that I did have *some* control over what had happened. Of course there are always going to be things that happen in our life that are completely out of our personal control, but what I was learning was that there is a lot more that we *can* control (or at least influence) than we usually realize. Accepting that I had "drawn" a bad relationships or bad situation into my life was one thing, but drawing an actual physical illness to me? I don't know. I certainly didn't do it consciously that's for sure. But were there choices that I had made, situations that I had been living in, stress that I could have handled better or maybe done things to avoid, were there things I did to my body or didn't do *for* my body, that helped "draw" IC into my life?

It's kind of scary when we first realize how powerful we are, how much we influence what is going on in our lives and in our bodies. It's a huge responsibility. But it is also a wonderful gift. Being made in the likeness and image of God, being made as creative beings with free will and choice, we have been given the tools within the universal laws to create whatever we wish in our lives. Part of my awakening on a spiritual level was about me learning to live my life more consciously, to pay more attention to how and what I was creating in my life. But this didn't come until later. First I was much too busy examining my past and what had brought me to the point of having a severe case of IC.

Obviously there are people who get sick and then get better without ever delving into their psyche and analyzing everything in their life. But maybe they healed on these other levels indirectly. Whether they had surgery, took medication, or just got better naturally, maybe at the same time, without really doing it "on purpose" or even realizing it, due to their illness they changed things in their life in some way. Maybe they healed things with a relative, started taking better care of their body (or their spirit), changed jobs, started exercising or whatever. Or maybe they didn't heal anything at all on a spiritual or emotional level. Maybe they just pushed the negative emotions down further and covered them up just as a medication can cover up physical symptoms. OR, maybe there just weren't any emotional or spiritual issues that needed healing. I mean...not everything has to have some big underlying psychological or spiritual message...does it?

At first I didn't understand why there had to be some big underlying psychological reason for why I had IC. Why couldn't it just be that there were physical reasons? And the answer, of course, is that it can be, if that is all we want to look at. Just because there is a connection between our mind, our body, and our spirit, doesn't mean we have to address it. And just because there are reasons on every level (physical, emotional, and spiritual) for every illness, does not mean that we have to look at them. It is totally a matter of choice. And even though I was choosing to look, there was one thing in particular that bothered me. It was hard for me to believe that everyone who had the same illness had the exact same psychological or spiritual reasons behind their being sick. Take the anger message for example. Just because one of the symbolic meanings of bladder problems is anger, does that mean everyone who has IC is angry? Obviously IC patients are not all angry about the same thing. But are we all angry about *something*? And if we are, how do we know what it is we are angry about if we don't even feel like we're angry?

Some people don't believe that there is an underlying spiritual and/or emotional reason for every illness. They believe that some things just happen by accident, that there doesn't have to be some big underlying reason for everything. I thought that at first too, but then I thought, if there is a spiritual or emotional reason for some illness, why is there not for others? It only made sense to me that there either is or there isn't a connection between physical illness and what is going on in our mental, emotional, and spiritual health. I know some people feel very judged to look at illness this way. And initially I know it's tough to get away from the whole judgment aspect. But it does gets easier when you realize that addressing the connection between the mind, body and spirit does not make the physical symptoms or the physical causes any less real. And when you realize that there is a connection for *all* illness, not just the ones that the medical community initially deems "all in the head", it becomes easier to see that it's not about judgment or blame. It is not about IC being an "emotional" illness caused by our psyche. It's about whatever messages, lessons, and/or gifts that we will receive from our IC. It's about using our IC as an opportunity for greater self-awareness and for the growth of our soul.

I had to be able to look at myself honestly when looking at the symbolic meaning of my symptoms. This is not an easy thing to do. It's not fun to examine our past mistakes and/or our emotional pain. It's sometimes hard to admit to ourselves that we feel a certain way about something. It can be so much easier to stay in denial, to not feel the pain and the guilt. But I knew that that was not going to help me to heal. It took courage for me to look at the truth, to admit to myself that I might have had something to do with why I got sick. It takes courage to be responsible for what is occurring in our life, to admit or realize that on some level we might have created the situation we are in whatever the situation (or illness). It takes courage to consider the possibility that in some sense we may have drawn it to us, whether consciously or subconsciously, by how we were leading our life, by what we were thinking, by how we were allowing others to treat us, and probably most significantly, by how we were treating ourselves. It is not easy.

And I'll tell you something else. Thinking is difficult. Facing our feelings is difficult. Making choices is difficult. That's why a lot of people don't do these things. They are not easy things to do. With IC, I knew I had to make the tough choices. I knew I had to do the thing that was not so easy to do. I knew I had to face some things that I really didn't want to face. And I knew that I had to make some changes in my life if I was going to get better. The first thing I had to learn was that I count.

I told this story in *To Wake In Tears*. One day when I was being particularly self critical, Charlie got upset with me and grabbed a piece of paper and wrote the words "I count" in big letters on it. Then he hung it up where I would see it all the time. I had gotten so used to hearing criticism that I had sort of taken over where others had left off. My thoughts and words about myself were often self-critical. Actually, once I started paying attention, I was kind of shocked at how often throughout the day my thoughts and words were self-critical. Fortunately for me it drove Charlie nuts to hear me talk that way so he was a wonderful reminder to me to be nicer to myself. Charlie really helped me to learn that I matter and that my feelings matter. That I was normal to have the feelings I had, that I was justified in having them, and that I should not be embarrassed about feeling hurt. I used to be too embarrassed to say to someone "you hurt my feelings". I think I saw it as a weakness, just as I saw my sensitivity my whole life. As a weakness to be overcome, to be ignored, to be stifled, so that things didn't hurt so much when they happened. If someone was mean to me, if a boyfriend cheated on me, if a friend disappointed me or someone said mean things behind my back, whatever it was that happened that hurt my feelings, I would try to push it down and not feel it. I didn't *want* to be sensitive. I was often told when I was young that I was "too sensitive". I was told that the intuitive feelings that I was picking up about other people were "wrong" or that I was just "exaggerating" or "imagining" it. In other words it was "all in my head". I find it very symbolic that I grew up to get a disease where I was told that it was "all in my head". Anyway, with IC, I began to learn to use my sensitivity to help me. Instead of ignoring or discounting my feelings, with IC, I learned that not only are my feelings important, they were actually my best guide when looking for answers on how to heal. My feelings more than mattered. They were absolutely essential to my figuring things out and healing on every level. With IC, I began to reawaken my intuitive side and get back in touch with my feelings.

As I've mentioned, I spent thousands of hours alone when I was sick so I had the opportunity for a lot of self-reflection and a lot of prayer and meditation. But before I ever started meditating, (okay don't laugh) I used to color on these giant posters with magic markers (poster art I think they call it) or sometimes I would play video games like Tetris (both things I could do on the bed) and for me they were a form of meditation. Doing something mindless allowed me the opportunity to think. I used to be able to do that when I exercised. Running especially was very meditative to me but I had stopped doing that after college. I had lost touch with what I was truly feeling and thinking because I had lost that meditative space that I used to allow myself. So as I colored on my posters with my heating pad faithfully attached to my bladder, I would think about things. I would think about the spiritual concepts I was reading about and about my life thus far. I would think about how I felt about things that had happened to me, how I felt about the people in my life, and how I felt about myself. This solitude, though at times sad and brutal, ended up being another gift I received from my IC. And though the self-reflection was not always a pretty sight, in the end it was a path for me to heal my emotions and my spirit, to heal things I didn't even know needed healing.

There were so many things I didn't realize needed healing, so many things that I didn't want to face. For example, before and even while I was sick, I found that I was rationalizing some of my behaviors and denying some of my feelings. Some things that I was doing that I could say were good for me (or helping me), in reality, at the very same time, were actually things that were also hurting me. Smoking, for example, I could rationalize and tell myself that with all the stress I was under being sick (and everything else) that smoking was comforting, that it was helping me to deal with the stress. If I was upset, afraid, angry, or whatever, I would smoke a cigarette and it would make me feel better.

But in reality, of course, it was also hurting me. And of course I knew that, but for a long time I conveniently ignored that part. It was the same with eating. When I was first sick I lost tons of weight and I was eating a lot of sugar foods and fattening (not too healthy) foods just to gain some weight back. On one level I knew it wasn't good for me, but I rationalized that I needed to put on some weight and that somehow made it okay. I didn't want to face quitting smoking and I didn't want to face changing my diet either. I also didn't want to face some of my feelings.

I didn't really want to face that I might be angry. I think many people, especially women, are raised to look at anger as something negative. After all, we don't want people to think we're a bitch or anything, do we? We want to be the "nice girls" that we were taught to be. Expressing anger is not something we are used to doing. In fact, some of us are so used to suppressing our anger and not speaking up for ourselves that sometimes we don't even realize it when we feel it! I know I didn't realize I was angry and I certainly didn't act like I was. I was aware that I was hurt though (not that I wanted to face that either). There is nearly always hurt beneath anger. Many times we end up feeling angry, rather than hurt, because it's a lot less painful to feel angry, although both are damaging emotions to the body. And actually, I now realize that I was truly feeling both. Even though I knew that there were definitely physical reasons for why I got sick, I still had to face the possibility that these emotions might have had something to do with my getting IC.

We can look at the symbolic meaning of our various symptoms, but obviously that doesn't offer us a clear-cut answer to "why me?" either. The symbolic meanings of our symptoms are not going to be specific to our personal situation. They do, however, offer us a starting point to explore our own individual life situation and our own inner truth. But remember that there is often more than one meaning for a particular symbol (or symptom) and the message or meaning of that symbol (or symptom) is not going to be exactly the same for each person. This is very important. Symbols are what they mean to you, not what they mean to someone else. That's what I meant by only you can know why you have IC or why you have ANY symptom. Only you can know inside what it is that's the issue or message for you. And by the way, sometimes we're not ready to see or understand the message yet. That's how it was for me with the anger message. It took some time and some self-reflection for me to understand because at first I just could not see it at all.

As I started to examine myself for what I could possibly be angry about, I realized that I did feel angry about certain things since *getting* IC. Obviously I wasn't too thrilled with the fact that I had it. I knew that initially I was angry with the particular doctors that I had seen. You know, for their ineptness, their lack of compassion, the fact that they physically hurt me and for the fact that they didn't believe me when I said something was wrong. I knew for certain that I was angry with the people in my life that thought I was crazy, people who thought I wasn't even physically sick and that it was "all in my head". I could see how I was angry about those things, but what the heck was I so angry about BEFORE I got sick? At first, that was what I didn't understand.

When I first got sick, I instantly blamed it on the moment (the surgery) without really reflecting much on what had happened before that. I did this for three reasons. One reason was that I didn't have any symptoms that I was aware of before that surgery. Secondly, my symptoms were so dramatic and so horrible immediately following the surgery (as in right when I woke up in the recovery room) that it was only logical for me to blame the surgery. And thirdly, I didn't realize that all that had gone on in my life *before* had any real bearing on what had happened *since* the surgery. I just wasn't looking at it from that perspective at all. Yet, as I said earlier, once I took a little time to look at it, I could see that there really *were* signs along the way. There were signs in my life and there were physical signs from my body, though brilliantly, I had ignored them all.

As I looked back on my life before I got IC, I guess it wasn't all that difficult to see why I got sick. For example, on a physical level, it was easy to see how my immune system became compromised immediately prior to getting IC. First there was the physical stress of having two surgeries within a two and a half week period. And then there was the time in between the two surgeries where I was in a lot of pain, barely getting any sleep, not being able to eat much, having a severe allergic reaction to a pain medication, and being afraid and stressed out from not knowing what was wrong and also from not being believed by the doctors (or anyone else for that matter). It was only logical that my immune system would be compromised. Even before I had the first surgery, I know my immune system was already somewhat compromised. I was under a lot of emotional stress. I probably wasn't eating right or getting enough rest. And then, looking farther back, knowing what I now know about my IC, I could see that the birth control pills I took when I was in my twenties, the antibiotics I took at various times in my life, the mercury/poison that was in my mouth via my fillings, and the fact that I was smoking cigarettes which are full of poisons and chemicals, all of these I now realize could have contributed to my lowered immune system and to why I ended up with IC. There were even more reasons that my immune system was in a weakened state by the time I got sick. Reasons that I had never even looked at before as having anything to do with my physical health.

It was the fall of 1991 (three years before I got sick) and I was just married to a guy that I had been seeing for over six years. I started a new job at a medical equipment company, which in many ways I was over qualified for. I took the job anyway because I needed the benefits and the money. For the next three years things would get worse and worse for me. My first marriage became a verbally and emotionally abusive relationship almost immediately upon returning home from the honeymoon. This was somewhat of a shock to me because I had been with this person for six years and it hadn't been like that. At the same time, I have to admit, there had been *some* signs. Again, I had brilliantly ignored them. So I went along and did what I thought I was supposed to do. Even though in my gut, I knew things weren't right, I did nothing to change things. The pressure of being married and starting his own business was my first husband's reasons for getting so critical and controlling about everything. Meanwhile, at work, because I was over qualified for the position I had been hired for, I was quickly promoted. Unfortunately, I was promoted over many of the other women in the office who had been there much longer than I had and this became an excuse for them to hate me. So within a fairly short amount of time my home life and work life both became abusive. At work, a few of the women (actually I should call them girls) were actually writing down every time I went to the bathroom and how long it took me. They were keeping a log and hoping to get me in trouble with it. It didn't work, but just the fact that they tried it was hurtful and such a violation of my privacy. I found the log at one point and was with two other managers at the time. They told me that these women were idiots and I should just forget about it and put it back where I found it. I was told to ignore them, which I did because I honestly didn't know what else to do. Meanwhile at home I was being criticized for nearly everything I did. I found myself constantly apologizing at home because I was always getting "scolded" for one thing or another. And even though I tried to stick up for myself, it didn't really matter. Very gradually, little by little, my self-esteem was being whittled down. My feelings were getting hurt on a regular basis and I really didn't do much about it for over two years.

It was in July of 1993, exactly one week after I turned thirty years old, that everything changed. I was at work one day and got a phone call from my mom. My mom had never called me at work before so I knew right away that something was wrong. It was my dad. He had had a stroke/heart attack and died suddenly. He was 55 years old and this was totally unexpected. I stayed in shock for a long time after. You know how when something hurts so much emotionally, you can barely even think about it for two minutes because it's just way too big? That's how it was for me after my dad died. The sadness was just way too big for me to feel it. I could only handle feeling it in very, very small pieces. I remember that day at the hospital. I took my first husband outside and told him that this was it. He would have no choice but to learn to be nice to me because now my dad could hear him. I felt that now that he had died, he would be able to hear and see what was going on. I knew my dad had not raised me to allow someone to talk to me the way my first husband was talking to me. I was ashamed and embarrassed that I had let things get so bad. Still it took me several months to get my act together and leave. It was one of the hardest things I ever had to do because I truly did love my first husband and I didn't want to break my vow to him. Mostly, I just didn't want to leave him alone. Strangely enough, I felt bad for him. I knew that he didn't mean to hurt me and I knew that he loved me. But I also knew that for my own sanity, my own health and well-being, I absolutely had to leave.

Leaving was a huge act of self-love for me. It was the first time in a long time that I had really stuck up for myself and put myself first. My happiness, my feelings, my physical and emotional well-being, all of them had been on the back burner. I didn't mean for them to be, it just sort of happened gradually. I realize now, looking back, that I had changed, that I really didn't even "feel like myself" even before I got sick with IC. Not like with the more recent anxiety symptoms I've described, but in terms of my confidence and self-esteem. When someone you love (and who supposedly loves you) constantly criticizes you, puts you down, and hurts your feelings, it's only natural to begin doubting yourself. It doesn't matter if they are a spouse, a parent, a sibling or a very close friend. Anyone who we care about what they think of us can have this effect on us. Little by little, one piece at a time, I was losing myself on a spiritual (or soul) level and this in turn weakened me physically. I was spending too much of my energy trying to be what my first husband wanted me to be (and not doing a very good job of it either I might add). There was negative energy around me and also from within me from my own thoughts about my job and my marriage.

Before I got sick with IC, I had been doing things and allowing things to happen in my life that were hurtful to me. Why? Because maybe on some kind of subconscious level, I felt like I deserved it...? I don't know. I do know that I must have felt something like that or why would I have stayed with someone who was being mean to me verbally, someone who was making me feel so bad inside? From one perspective I can blame it all on him believing that it was wrong how he treated me. But, especially from my new perspective, I could see that there was more to it than that.

At some point I had to face that I had allowed all of this to happen to me. And that was what was so upsetting. It had been me. I had been the one who had let other people mistreat me. Hell...I had mistreated myself. As much as I could pinpoint certain situations and certain people who had hurt me or done mean things to me, I had been the one who had allowed it to happen. I had ignored my needs for the needs of others. I had ignored my feelings, caring more about other people's feelings than my own. I had allowed toxic people into my life and it had greatly affected me. And I knew it was affecting me even *while* it was affecting me, but I didn't do anything to change it. It was me who stayed in a bad relationship and allowed myself, simply by staying in it, to be mistreated. It was me who had stayed in a job situation where I was being taken advantage of and mistreated. And THIS was truly where my anger was. My anger was with myself. I had to face that I was not only angry with the people who had mistreated me, but *most of all* at myself who had allowed it.

Everything outside of us is a reflection of what is going on inside of us. This spiritual truth took the universal law of attraction ("like attracts like") and the law of karma ("what goes around, comes around") to a whole new level for me. What I learned is that "what goes around, comes around" applies not only to how we treat other people, but sometimes even more importantly, to how we treat ourselves. Both of these universal laws help determine what we "draw to us". I knew that I had been attracting people into my life who were mean to me. Why? Because I was being mean to myself. I had always thought other people "did things to me". I never looked at it as if they were doing to me what *I* was doing to me.

We all have choices to make, every day, that determine the course of our lives. I had been making the wrong choices, the self-destructive choices. Not consciously of course. I was not consciously trying to self-destruct, but subconsciously, apparently, I was. Sometimes, when our life is off track, God/the Universe seems to step in and sort of slap us in the face (so to speak) or shake up our world somehow. Sometimes, if we don't pay attention to the smaller signs, something big will happen that feels like it shatters us into a million pieces and all of a sudden everything is different. And when that happens, we have a choice. We can either let it break us or we can rise back up and face the world again within our new situation (which for us, is IC).

What's funny is that in my case, I actually DID get slapped in the face when this all started. When I look back and realize when I first started taking a turn, changing my life, and going in the wrong direction, I literally got slapped in the face with a baseball bat. I told this story in my other books because this was what broke some of my teeth that had mercury fillings. I was playing softball with a bunch of friends from college when a bat broke, flew across the field and hit me right across the right side of my face. That event, like many other "accidents" in our lives, held much meaning for me, both physically and symbolically. Physically, I'm sure I had a greater susceptibility to having the mercury/poison in my fillings affect my health due to the broken teeth that had big fillings. And symbolically, it was my "big slap in the face". It was God/the Universe trying to get my attention.

But I wasn't hearing the message. I wasn't even trying to listen. At the time, I didn't realize it was a sign. I didn't know it was a warning. And even though it took several more years, eventually I got an even bigger "slap in the face" when I got IC. With IC, I was sort of forced to wake up and start paying attention. If I wanted to rise back up and face the world again, if I wanted to heal from IC and all the other symptoms I got with it, I had to start paying more attention.

So anyway, there I was, not ten months after my dad passed away, alone in my new apartment with only a mattress on the floor, a phone, a small color television that my dad had sent me my freshman year in college, and some of my clothes. It was only a couple months later that I got the cyst on my ovary that started my whole IC nightmare. When I had the surgery to remove or drain the cyst, the doctor missed it and removed several smaller cysts. The next day after my doctor had left for vacation, the huge cyst ruptured. It took two and a half weeks to convince her associates that something was wrong. Eventually when I learned that I had a ruptured cyst that was bleeding into the abdominal cavity, I called my boss and told him I'd have to go back in for a second surgery. He ignored the severity of the situation and told me that he'd see me on Monday and hung up. It was Friday, so he expected me to come in to work with only two days to recover. He was angry because I had missed so much time during the two and half weeks prior. That was the final straw. I was going to have the surgery, get better and search for a new job immediately. I had had enough of those nasty women anyway. Unfortunately, that second surgery was the one where I woke up in the recovery room with symptoms of IC. Of course at the time I had no idea what IC was or what was wrong with me. So there I was physically sick, I had just left my first husband and now I was searching for a new job while still working in a miserable situation. Fortunately I found another job rather quickly. I was thrilled to leave my old job, but it was still stressful to be starting something new. As I was learning the in's and out's of my new job, I was in the horrendous process of trying to get diagnosed. I was completely stressed out. The only light in my life at that point was Charlie. Even though we were just friends at that time, he was the most supportive, understanding, and helpful friend I had ever had. It was because he was there that I would begin to heal.

Although I spent a lot of time alone while I was sick, I was also extremely fortunate to have Charlie to talk to about everything. When he wasn't at work or out of town on business (which thank God didn't happen all that often), we had time together to talk. I was able to discuss with him all the choices I was about to make in terms of how to treat my IC and about all the choices I had made in the past that may have led me to getting sick in the first place. I think everyone needs someone to talk to as they are trying to understand why they got IC because it's not going to be a simple answer, not on a physical, emotional or spiritual level.

Even though there was so much we couldn't do together because of my IC, Charlie and I felt such gratitude for the opportunity we had (because of my IC) for such quality time together. We had time to get to know each other on a soul level, to understand how each other felt about things, and to discover how we came to be the people we are today. We learned together the power of gratitude quite accidentally simply because it came to us so naturally. We were so grateful to God that we had found each other and so grateful for the opportunity to be together. It didn't matter that we didn't have material abundance back then (or even that I had IC) because we knew that we had what was most important. We had unconditional love between us. Love without conditions placed on it is probably the most valuable, the most precious gift we can ever give or receive. We knew we were fortunate and we couldn't help but feel and express our gratitude. Even though I was sick and there was a lot we couldn't do together because of it, we were still happy. I know this must sound weird to some people, but we couldn't help it. Even in the midst of my physical suffering we were able to see how blessed we were. By concentrating on what we *did* have and believing that we already *had* everything, we automatically drew more and more of the same wonderful abundance to us. We were using the universal law of attraction without even realizing it. The universal law of attraction is (simply put) "like attracts like". What we focus on, we draw to us. When we focus on good things, we draw more good things to us. When we focus on negative things, we draw more negative things to us. As you shift your focus to what you have, you give the universe "permission" to send you more.

Ironically, in terms of my healing, it all started with gratitude. I was the most grateful to, and for, Charlie who took care of me when I could not, not only physically, but also financially and emotionally. I knew I was fortunate to have someone who believed me that something was physically wrong, someone who knew that I wasn't crazy or just some stressed out, emotional female. Even the bad experiences I had with the doctors I was quickly able to be grateful for because that is what led me to treating myself, which really was how I ended up getting better. I also looked at it like "forgive them, they know not what they do", because I do believe that those urologists and doctors out there who are hurting IC patients really don't intend to. They are just doing what they know how to do. They truly "don't know any better". So from that perspective it was really the easiest of all for me to forgive the doctors. It was much more difficult for me to forgive the people closer to me. As I've said before, it wasn't at all easy for me to deal with the emotional hurt of not having people believe me (or care) that I was physically sick. As one of my IC friends put it, it is SO painful that it is literally soul destroying to have the people who we thought cared about us treat us as if our IC were no big deal or not even real. It took some time before I could be grateful for their disbelief and indifference, but eventually I looked at it like, at least now I know who really cares about me. A lot of people never have that opportunity.

It came very naturally and without any effort at all for me to be grateful for each step I made along the way of getting better. As much as the setbacks were disappointing and frustrating, I tried always to focus on the improvements. Yes there were times I cried and times I felt depressed or sorry for myself. I think that's only normal and to be expected. But because I knew that thoughts are things, I did my best to concentrate, for the most part, on the positive. After all, I still had so much to be grateful for. I can still remember how much I appreciated it the first time I could take a shower without pain, the first time I could walk up and down the stairs without holding onto the railing in pain, the first time I could go to the bathroom and know that it wasn't going to hurt, the first time I could start eating foods and drinking things that I used to love but couldn't have when I was sick, the first time I could ride in a car where the vibrations didn't kill my bladder. I could go on and on. The more I thanked God/the Universe for me getting better, the more it drew more "getting better" to me. That's the beauty of gratitude. Thanking God for my good health was my way of saying to the Universe that I already HAD good health. Thoughts are energy. What we believe, we become. And as I sent this energy, this belief that I was already healthy, out into the Universe, the more it helped draw "healthiness" to me.

Gratitude is a choice. Choosing to look on the bright side, choosing to see the good in a bad situation, and focusing on what we still have to be grateful for is definitely a choice. A lot of times it seems much easier to be negative about things. And it can be. It's much easier to complain and blame other people or blame circumstances. But that choice, the choice to see things negatively, not only takes all the responsibility away from us, it is also a choice that will influence our future reality. It is a choice that will create more negativity in our lives. What we focus on, we get more of. That's just the way it works. And even though it can take a little more effort to choose to look on the positive side, it is well worth it when we recognize the impact it has on our future moments. Of course, taking the time to be grateful can be difficult when physically we feel horrible. But gratitude is especially beneficial during times of pain and illness. We can offer our illness and pain back to the Divine in prayer with deep appreciation and gratitude for the gifts of Spirit the illness is offering. We might not know what the gifts are yet, but we can choose to receive our illness with love and gratitude, knowing that there is a greater purpose, a greater spiritual purpose for the growth of our soul. This is what I chose to believe. And so, of course, this is what proved to be the case for me. What we believe is true in our minds, is true, whether we realize it or not.

Believing in the perfection even when we don't understand why something is happening to us, knowing that everything is as it should be in God's perfect world, even when from our perspective it does not appear that way, is a major act of faith. It takes faith to believe that everything that happens to us is for our highest good or for the growth of our soul, even when it's not readily apparent. Before I got sick, before I began to understand why IC came into my life, I had trouble having that faith. But now I can see that even bad things can turn out to be miracles. It's just that we might not realize it at the time. Sometimes the things we see as "bad", later we end up seeing as a "good" thing or even as a miracle that maybe saved us from a worse fate or taught us something invaluable that we may not have learned otherwise. Maybe the "bad" thing brought us to a place in our life where otherwise we would not be and in that way, the "bad" thing was really a "good" thing.

One thing I learned from having IC is that sometimes we don't recognize a miracle (or a message) even when it's staring us right in the face. How many of us have said "oh thank God" after something has happened and then we end up immediately brushing it off, forgetting, or maybe not even recognizing, that we just experienced a miracle? How many times have we discounted something that occurred considering it "just a coincidence" instead of recognizing it as a miracle?

What I learned is that there are miracles that happen every single day even in the midst of misery and tragedy. Every day we are here is a miracle and every person we come in contact with, (especially those we have a relationship with) and every "thing" we come across has a message for us. Once I started listening and paying attention, I started to see how true that really is. When we look at things from a perspective of gratitude, we automatically begin to see more miracles in our lives. As I began to notice all the "coincidences" that were leading me to answers in terms of my healing on a physical level, I started to realize that they weren't coincidences at all, but a series of miracles.

When we get to that point in our life where we realize that everything up until this moment was preparing us for this, our life's purpose or our destiny, then we start to also realize, that there is no such thing as coincidence. That first year after being diagnosed I had read *The Celestine Prophecy* by James Redfield. It is about a man who is on a physical journey and learns certain spiritual insights along the way. Reading that book helped me to start seeing the coincidences in my own life and how they weren't coincidences at all, how all that had happened before in my life brought me to this point. I could see how the seemingly bad things that had happened to me were for a reason, a greater purpose. Once I realized that I was to write *To Wake In Tears* and try to help IC patients, I could look back on my life and see why some of the things happened to me as they did. For example, now I could see why I ended up going to the college I went to even though when I was going there I had no idea why I had ended up there and even felt as if I had gone to the wrong place. I went to a small liberal arts college called Kenyon College. It was a small school (smaller in enrollment than my high school) that looked like it was plucked out of England and plopped down on a big hill in the middle of farm country in Ohio. While I was there I had no idea what I was doing there. Not only was it totally un-me to be in this small town atmosphere, the academics were much tougher than I had anticipated. Needless to say, I had always thought I had made a wrong choice. Now I can see that it wasn't a coincidence at all that I ended up at a school renowned for its' English Literature department, a school that taught me how to write. I could have never written my books had I not gone to Kenyon College.

I don't believe it was a coincidence that I grew up with a mom who (beginning at least 35 years ago) was into vitamins and herbs and a dad who was into metaphysics long before these were "popular" things to be "into". I don't think it was a coincidence that I worked at a job (which in many respects was not at all right for me) where I ended up learning all about computers right before I got sick. I don't believe it was a coincidence that I grew up with three brothers and no sisters, where I spent the majority of my free time playing sports instead of playing with dolls. I don't believe it was a coincidence that I grew up constantly being told that I could do anything I set my mind to. I could not have gotten better from IC otherwise. I would not have had the open mindedness toward alternative treatments, the understanding of how important our attitude is, the physical toughness to get into the pool and swim when I was swollen and in pain, even the ability to get on line and talk to other IC patients or write books about IC, I could not have done any of it had I not had the experiences I had in my life.

With gratitude and seeing the connections, I began to see the Divine in everything. Everything that had happened in my life thus far and everything that was happening in the present started to make more sense to me. I was able to see the perfection or at least understand that things were perfect even when they didn't appear that way in the moment. I started watching for the signs and trying to understand what God/the Universe was telling me. At some point I got really into it. I learned the symbolic meaning of various colors, numbers, animals, birds, and insects. They all have symbolic meanings and it was so fun and interesting to me to watch what was crossing my path. Even when I was alone most of the time and couldn't go anywhere, I *still* got messages. Sometimes they would come through what I saw out the window of my bedroom, sometimes through a person on the phone or something I read in a book or saw on television. I remember back in college reading books, plays, and poems (even watching movies) and then analyzing and discussing the symbolism contained in them. And now, here I was, doing it in my life in much the same way. I was watching for the symbols, looking for the coincidences, and trying to understand the messages that were right there in front of me.

I was learning a whole new way to communicate with God/the Universe. Or I should say, I was learning a whole new way that God/the Universe was communicating with me. I found it very empowering to experience this new form of communication and this new, expanded understanding of how to apply the universal laws to my own life. I also found that once I became aware of the "coincidences" and connections, once I became conscious of the symbols, not only the messages my body was sending me, but also the messages God/the Universe was sending (and had been sending all along), my life changed. I could no longer look at my symptoms the same way anymore. I could no longer see my IC (or any of the other chronic illnesses that had developed with my IC) as simply physical diseases.

This is how and why I went back to reading about the mind/body/spirit connection. This is how and why I went back to examining the symbolic message of my IC symptoms.

Looking at things from the perspective that each symptom has some symbolic psychological meaning, I appeared to be some kind of emotional wreck!! Well, not really. We all have emotional pain from our past that we carry with us, whether consciously or subconsciously. It doesn't mean that we have "emotional problems" or even that we feel unhappy. What was weird for me was that by the time I was diagnosed with IC, I was already very happy again with my life (mostly because of Charlie and also because I had switched jobs). But that didn't mean that I was all the way over all the hurt feelings from the years before getting sick. It didn't mean that I had forgiven myself for putting myself in those situations or for not getting out of them sooner. It didn't mean that my emotional pain had not become manifest in my physical body.

It was true that I had been in emotional pain from my first marriage, from the situation at my job, and most of all, from missing my dad. And it was true that what I had been doing with my life was definitely not in agreement with my spirit. But I did not get IC because I was in a bad marriage or because I was being mistreated at work. And I did not get IC because my dad died or because of the emotional pain it caused me to lose him. This I can tell you for certain. It was not any *one thing* that caused me to get IC. Not on a physical, emotional, or spiritual level. I got IC for a multitude of reasons. Just like for most all illness, there were multiple reasons on multiple levels and it was the combination of all of them that resulted in my getting IC. Actually, to put it quite simply, I believe I got IC because my body was out of balance, my emotions were out of balance, and so was my life.

"How I've learned to please
To doubt myself in need
You'll never, you'll never know."
- Natalie Merchant "Stockton Gala Days"

Chapter 8

Finding Balance

You would think I would have gotten good at this by now after doing it for all of my other symptoms, but apparently not. As it turned out, the signs, the answers to my remaining symptoms, were there all along, but it took me nearly two years to see them. I was so close to it that I couldn't see the forest for the trees (as they say). At least I knew one thing during that time. I knew that somehow I must still be out of balance.

I've known for a long time now that healing from IC is about getting the body back in balance. It's how I had gotten better so far. Heck, I even wrote about it in my first two books. So I knew that I must still be out of balance somehow or I wouldn't have these remaining symptoms. But *how* was I out of balance? That was the million-dollar question.

Just as we had always tried to understand the mystery of my IC symptoms, for the next several months (after *To Wake In Tears* came out) Charlie and I tried to figure out what was causing the remaining edema/swelling and the intense anxiety which seemed mysteriously connected to IBS-like symptoms. At first I thought that the leftover edema was related to a sodium/potassium imbalance. I took a potassium supplement for a while and it did help. The swelling went down further, but it wasn't the whole answer. There was something else going on. Charlie was always telling me that swimming and exercise would help with the anxiety by bringing back my confidence in my body and in myself. We both hoped it would also help with the swelling. And even though swimming and working out was helping me in several ways, it didn't seem to be the answer for the leftover edema/swelling either. I knew some of my swelling had gone down by eliminating my allergies with NAET and of course more had gone down as I was detoxing from the mercury fillings, but it hadn't gone away completely, so it remained a mystery. One thing I did notice was that the most change in my swelling would occur with each menstrual cycle as I would swell up more before and then shrink more after (not just in the pelvic area, but all over). I had no idea how or why, but I seemed to be shrinking a little bit more each month.

In terms of the anxiety, it was difficult to know how much of my symptoms were physical and how much were psychological. Charlie and I talked about it all the time as things came up that I would get nervous about doing and also as I would get sick for no apparent reason, when there was nothing at all causing me to be nervous. It was really hard for me not to blame myself even though I *knew* there was definitely a physical aspect to it. I guess it just seemed like I should be able to control it somehow. And I guess I believed that other people must think that as well.

How weird is it that I was again dealing with something that appeared to be in my head? First I get IC, no one believes me or understands what it is, and they tell me it's in my head. Now I have this anxiety and in many ways I feel it's physical but I know it appears to be psychological. Obviously there is some kind of message in there for me. And now, as I write this, I realize what it is. It's about me learning to believe in myself again, to believe in my feelings, to trust them and to act on them. I have to believe in myself enough to know that it is NOT just in my head, that it is NOT just psychological. Just like with the IC when I had to believe in myself and trust my own perception of my own body, my own perception of my physical symptoms, enough to continue going from doctor to doctor to find out what was wrong. It's the same with the anxiety. I had to keep on searching for the physical explanation. I had to stop blaming myself. I knew there was more to it than the psychological part, even if I could see that the psychological was playing a role. (It's always a combination thing anyway.) I felt there *must* be a physical explanation for the anxiety not only because it was so out of control and so un-me to be this way, but also because I should be able to be nervous, psychologically speaking, without it making me physically sick.

To be honest, initially it didn't occur to me that the *psychological* part of the anxiety and fear that I was feeling could actually be being caused by a physical imbalance. It was really my mom who kept telling me that I still must have had a physical imbalance of some kind or else I wouldn't be feeling this type of anxiety. Of all people, it was my mom telling me that it wasn't my fault, that it wasn't in my head or being caused by something "in my head". I say "of all people" because it was my mom who used to tell me that I was "too sensitive" when I was a kid (not to be mean of course but because she didn't want me to get hurt so easily) and it was my mom who used to tell me that what I was feeling was "my imagination" or "an exaggeration" (again, not to be mean, but because she just didn't see whatever or whoever it was in the same way that I did). So it was ironic that it was my mom who was now trying to tell me that this wasn't an exaggeration or my imagination, it wasn't "just psychological" and it wasn't my fault for feeling this way. IC offered me an amazing opportunity to heal things with my mom. And this, her trying to convince me that I wasn't "crazy" regarding the fear and anxiety, that it was being caused by something physical and not something in my head, this, was wonderful evidence to me of our healing things between us, of both of us changing our perspective of each other. The confirmation my mom provided me helped pushed me forward to examine the possible physical causes of my IC related anxiety.

All of this was happening, by the way, as I began my second book. This was also about the same time I began to understand that the mind/body/spirit connection is not just about how our emotions can affect our health. It also works the other way around. *Our physical health can also affect our emotions.* A chemical or nutritional imbalance in the body can cause feelings of depression or anxiety.

101

They are feelings we seem to have no control over because they are actually being caused by something physical.

Once I began to research what happens to the body under stress and discovered the physical connection between stress and IC (that I wrote about in *Along the Healing Path*) things started to make some sense. Just as a quick review or in case you haven't read *Along the Healing Path*... When we are under any kind of emotional or physical stress, our adrenal glands, or stress glands as they are often referred to, release certain chemicals and hormones to help our body deal with the stress. Because our body cannot distinguish between physical and emotional stress, our adrenals respond the same way regardless of the actual cause of the stress. Not only do many IC patients note that they were under tremendous emotional and/or physical stress at the onset of their IC, many also notice that stress definitely increases their IC symptoms. In my opinion, when you have IC, whether you were under emotional and/or physical stress at the onset of it or not, you are more than likely experiencing both types of stress on the body now that you *have* IC. Just having IC can be very stressful emotionally and it is definitely stressful physically. The problem is that the adrenal glands need vitamin C and all the B vitamins in order to function properly. As you probably already know, IC patients generally cannot tolerate taking vitamin C or B vitamins as they can both cause burning pain in the bladder. It is my opinion that most IC patients are not only sensitive to vitamin C and the B vitamins, but most of us are also deficient in both. Therefore an IC body is not as easily able to handle stress as a "normal" healthy body because we don't have the nutrients needed for our adrenal glands and body to deal with it. Just as stress and IC are linked on a physical level, so are anxiety and IC. In fact, anxiety is linked to IC on more than one level. Not only is anxiety a fairly common symptom among those with IC, interestingly enough it is also another symbolic message of the bladder.

Even though the anxiety symptom was a new thing for me, I now know that a lot of IC patients experience anxiety. And just like all of our other symptoms, we are not all going to be the same. Some IC patients might have only mild anxiety symptoms while others might experience panic attacks. There are some IC patients who experience no anxiety symptoms at all. I used to be among that group. Although I did notice, like most of us do, that stress and/or anxiety worsen our IC symptoms. And I know that for some IC patients, when they have a "flare" of their IC symptoms, they feel more anxiety symptoms. So the connection goes both ways. There are many IC patients who take anti-anxiety medications and though I can *completely* understand and relate to why they do (because it is so awful to feel this way and it restricts your life so very much), for me, I just wasn't comfortable taking it. As much work as I did to cleanse my body and eliminate anything synthetic, toxic, or chemical, I didn't want to risk introducing a synthetic chemical medication to my body. To be honest, I was too scared to take the medication. I was concerned about going backward in my healing. I felt I had to get to the root of the problem. I believed that there was an underlying physical cause to why I was having anxiety and I knew for certain that it was somehow connected to my IC. Again I would choose to listen to my body and myself over what the standard medical treatment would be.

So there I was trying to treat my anxiety problem with B vitamins. Of course, initially, I was afraid to just jump right in and start taking a B complex or a multiple vitamin. Even though my bladder was better, I was still nervous about doing it. (If you have IC, I know you understand.) Instead I found something that had all the B vitamins in it, something that was liquid, something that I could easily control the amount that I was going to take. I started drinking wheatgrass juice. Wheatgrass juice is rich in vitamins E, K, and B complex. It also contains lots of amino acids (proteins) and tons of minerals, including calcium, iron, magnesium, and potassium. All of the "green drinks" like wheatgrass juice, chlorella, and barley green contain chlorophyll, which is not only alkalizing to the system, but has also been shown to discourage bacteria growth. I drank wheatgrass juice for all of those reasons, but mostly because it is rich in B vitamins. I drank my B vitamins and minerals for the same reason I recommend using single herbs in tea form for treating IC. It is easier for the body to absorb and we can control how much of it we take. I could make it as weak as I liked and drink as little as I wanted to in order to make sure that it wasn't bothering me. It doesn't taste that great, but I got used to it. I drank it every day after lunch. It actually helped my intestines as well as my anxiety symptom, which for me certainly seemed to be connected. (By this time in my healing I was also able to drink orange juice and eat all kinds of fruit. This was primarily how I was getting my vitamin C.)

Eventually I was able to take a multiple vitamin that contained all the B's and a good amount of vitamin C in each. I started out slow, as I did with everything, and worked my way up to taking one a day. In my excitement, as I noticed it helping me so much, I increased my dose to two a day. It didn't bother my bladder at all, but all of a sudden I got a huge, horrible vulvodynia flare-up like none that I had ever experienced before. At the time I assumed it was because my body just couldn't handle that large of a dose. And of course, that was partly the reason. But *why* couldn't my body handle it and why did it bring out a huge flare in vulvodynia symptoms? What was the connection there? I wouldn't understand the answer to those questions for at least another year. At least at the time I knew enough to take a break from those vitamins, which of course I did mostly out of fear of another vulvodynia flare-up like that one.

After the whole B vitamin/stress connection I was still not back to normal, but it had definitely helped. I was a lot braver than I had been in terms of going places and I was experiencing less anxiety symptoms overall. Then all of a sudden the bonding fell off my tooth. All of the fears came rushing back when I realized that I would have to go to the dentist to get it fixed. Now I realize that petrified is a pretty strong word, but to be honest, even though it may sound like I'm exaggerating, I *swear* it's not a strong enough word to describe how I felt the morning of my appointment. I was scared, nervous, and worried the whole night before and had gotten very little sleep. I was up early that morning with horrible IBS symptoms, nausea, and that unpleasant, "going far away in my head" feeling. I wasn't sure if it was due to the anxiety/fear of having to go back to the dentist or if it was just a coincidence that I was *that* sick that particular morning. It's not like I hadn't gotten this sick before when I *wasn't* nervous. So again, just like on Mother's Day the year before, it was difficult to distinguish how much of my symptoms were being caused by the physical and how much was being caused by the psychological. I did recognize that I was definitely nervous psychologically speaking. After all I had been through with having my fillings replaced, all the bad experiences of having to sit through those appointments when I didn't feel good, I knew I was nervous about going back there. But I couldn't be sure if it was being nervous or if it was being caused by something physical that morning. I knew that it was much more than just a simple case of nervousness though. And I knew that what Charlie always says is true and it was probably "a combination thing".

Regardless, I felt like *such* an idiot for being so scared over a little nothing dentist appointment. I mean…I didn't even have to have a shot of Novocain or even get drilled or ANYTHING! I just had to sit in the chair for 10-15 minutes with my head back and my mouth open. That's it! But no matter how many times I told myself that in my head, it didn't help at all. Again my intellect, my mind, was not able to affect my physical body. I spoke to my mom on the phone that morning and she was still trying to tell me that it was a chemical imbalance in my body. Of course she had never seen me like this so she was pretty shocked and perplexed that I would be this petrified over going to an easy dentist appointment. Like the B vitamins, she insisted there must be another imbalance that I wasn't aware of. This had to be physical. It just didn't make any sense to us otherwise. At that point I was considering hypnosis or an emotional NAET treatment, but the morning of that appointment, I was stuck with those feelings of being scared shitless. Excuse my language, but I wanted to point out how symbolic that phrase is because that's exactly what would happen to me when I got scared. Anyway, I didn't end up going to the dentist that morning. I canceled my appointment and changed it to five days later. I had five days to get it together so that I could make it to the dentist and have the bonding taken care of.

My mom had been trying for quite some time to convince me to try Tahitian Noni juice. The main reason she wanted me to try it was because it is said to help provide a sense of well-being, among other things. Noni juice is a dietary supplement made from a fruit called Noni that has been growing in Tahiti for centuries. It has been used by the Tahitians to treat all kinds of ills. It is said to be good for inflammation and great for boosting the immune system. It is also cleansing to the colon and body. Even though it was helping my mom and other people she knew, I was afraid to try it because I thought it might bother my bladder or my intestines. So for a long time I didn't listen. But that morning, in the midst of feeling this out of control anxiety/fear, in the midst of being so sick physically, I finally decided that I would give it a try. I would start out with the smallest dosage imaginable. A small amount on my tongue to make sure it didn't bother me. The first time I tried it, even with that tiny of an amount, I got a reaction. I knew that with many natural products, getting a reaction the first time you use it can mean that you need it or that it will help you. It can work that way with vitamins too. Ironically, we usually have some type of reaction when taking the vitamins that are body needs most. I believe that's one of the reasons why IC patients cannot tolerate the B vitamins and vitamin C. Because these are the vitamins we are lacking and these are the vitamins we need the most. Anyway, that's how it was for me with the Noni juice. I took it the first time and it not only irritated the remaining blisters in my throat (from having the mercury in my mouth), it also bothered my intestines and made me feel sick. BUT, it definitely helped me feel calmer inside. There was no question that it helped me with the anxiety. I took it for the next five days, small doses of course, and I did end up making it to that dentist appointment.

Rebuilding my body with B vitamins and vitamin C helped my anxiety symptom by nourishing my adrenal glands with the nutrients they need to handle stress and in this way I was helping to rebalance my body. I did other things to rebalance my body as well. I started doing yoga, which surprisingly enough, even with the inflexibility caused by my swelling, I still ended up enjoying. Aside from the yoga, I was swimming and exercising on alternate days and drinking Noni juice. All of this was helping, but it wasn't enough. I still had swelling. My skin was still messed up. And though somewhat better, I still had the anxiety symptom that was still mysteriously connected to the IBS/going far away in my head/feeling nauseas/covered in a cold sweat symptom. (Can you tell I never know what to call it?)

At first we thought that as time passed, I would automatically get braver about going places. However, it didn't work out like that. In fact, as time went on, it seemed to be getting worse. Everyone was telling me that I should take baby steps. I should keep trying to go places and eventually I would be more comfortable. For me, this was the wrong approach. Maybe later down the line something like that might prove helpful, but at this point, it was not the answer for me. The more I tried to do, the more places I tried to go, the more bad experiences I had. Strangely enough, trying to face my fears was actually making them worse. At some point I realized that addressing the psychological aspects was not going to help me until the physical aspects were resolved. Yet still I was getting more and more frustrated and impatient with myself.

As I was down on myself for still not being better in terms of the anxiety I had to remind myself again that everything happens for a reason. That when I was ready on a spiritual/emotional level, then the physical answers would show up. That's how it worked for me the whole time I was healing from IC. Obviously, I wasn't ready yet to stop being afraid. Obviously there was a reason that I still had this anxiety problem. All along I felt it had something to do with my writing this book, though for a long time I didn't know exactly how or why. I had to believe that when I was ready, the answers would come and then I would know how to finish healing. And then I would also know the rest of what I was meant to put in this book.

107

Sure enough, when I was ready the answers did appear. As soon as I was ready to let it go and say...okay, I give up, I have no idea what to do anymore about this anxiety. I "gave it to God" as "they" say one night before going to sleep. I prayed and promised God that I would pay very close attention. I promised to watch and listen for signs knowing that He would provide them. I promised to continue doing everything I knew how to do and I would wait. I had to believe in the perfection knowing that if this continued, that there was a reason for it. I knew that when the time was right, the answers would come. I believe this is what "they" mean by surrender. What we resist persists. What we focus on, we get more of. Once we "let it be okay", it is much easier to let "it" go. Just as I had to let it be okay that I had IC, I had to let it be okay that I had this anxiety. If I was going to be this way the rest of my life, afraid to go places and do things for fear of getting sick and "going far away in my head", then that's *just the way it's going to be*.

It was about 8 months ago that I said that prayer and it was about 8 months ago that things started falling into place. Just like when I discovered the connection between my IC and my mercury fillings (and so many other things) as I was trying to get better, the signs were there all along. I was seeing them, but I hadn't realized that I was seeing them. I hadn't put them all together. I hadn't figured out the message. For some things, I admit, I didn't want to listen or I didn't want to make the effort. The mercury fillings are a good example. I didn't want to face what I knew was the truth, because I didn't want to go to the dentist. I knew that mercury was a poison. Heck, we all learn not to play with thermometers when we're kids. And I knew that whether or not the mercury in my fillings was effecting my IC symptoms or not, that it was not a good thing to have poison in my mouth. It was only logical. But I didn't want to spend the money or go through the aggravation of having my fillings replaced. Yet over and over again I kept coming across information regarding the dangers of mercury amalgam fillings as I was doing research on the Internet. Sometimes I would see articles at an alternative medicine website or sometimes I would just happen upon a website regarding something spiritual for example and run across links to information on mercury amalgam. I was told by several different people that it would be smart to have my fillings replaced, but I always blew it off thinking that I had a lot of fillings and it would be really hard to do it with being sick and all. I kept running across the word mercury. From mercury retrograde in astrology to the movie "Mercury Rising" (that was in theaters at the time) to hearing a commercial for a recording artist on Mercury Records, etc. It was in my face all the time until I was ready to listen. And that's how it can work sometimes. When the answers come we always have a choice whether to listen. It may take several times that God/the Universe gives us signs before we listen, before we take action, but we can't beat ourselves up about that. We shouldn't blame ourselves if we haven't been ready yet or if we haven't been listening. It will happen when we're ready and at the perfect time for each of us. Because everything is as it should be.

Everything is as it should be. I used to say that line over and over again when I was sick. When I was scared from a new symptom or even an old symptom that came back, I would tell myself that there was a reason. Even if I didn't understand what it was in that moment, I had to believe that there was a higher purpose, a message, a reason for what was happening. With all that was happening to me physically with my IC it was way too scary *not* to believe this. Having that faith, believing that everything is as it should be in every moment of time, helped me to accept what was going on with me and helped me to know that I would someday find an answer. Even though I felt it was my destiny to write about IC and spend my time trying to help other IC patients, I knew there was also a message more specifically for *me*, a higher message coming from my spirit. And I knew there was a message with the anxiety problem as well. I just had to figure out what it was.

The very next morning after I said that prayer 8 months ago, I was sitting in front of my computer like I usually do and it hit me. The idea just popped right into my head (as all inspiration from Spirit does). I typed all of my remaining symptoms, right in a row, in the search line of my favorite Internet search engine. And when I did, I remember thinking to myself, "Geez! Why didn't I think of this before?!". Anyway, what came up was astounding to me. I was shocked to see web page after web page of articles on low progesterone or what they call Estrogen Dominance. By this time in my healing journey, I have no idea why I was shocked. I had been getting all kinds of signs from the universe that there was a hormone connection with my IC.

A lot of people believe that there is a hormone connection with their IC. Many people notice an increase in their symptoms around ovulation or their menstrual cycle and many have "female problems" that started their IC problems. Some IC patients get ovarian cysts, fibroid tumors, and/or endometriosis, and many have had hysterectomies. Some people get IC immediately following a hysterectomy and others get hysterectomies thinking that it might help their IC symptoms. Many IC patients experience heavy periods, horrible cramps, bloating in the pelvic area, breast tenderness, hot flashes, etc. In fact, one of the signs I had been getting for months was from all the people who would ask me, after reading *To Wake In Tears*, what I thought about the hormone connection with IC because they believed that for them, there might be a connection. I would always apologize and explain that I was only in my thirties and I hadn't been through menopause or had a hysterectomy so I really didn't know all that much about hormones. (I had foolishly assumed that I didn't really need to know much about hormones until I was closer to menopause age. Boy was I wrong.) Anyway, I remember thinking that maybe I should read more about hormones because people kept asking me what I thought about it. But for some reason I didn't end up doing it at the time.

There were other signs as well. I knew that I felt more anxiety from mid-cycle (ovulation) until getting my period. I was also more afraid to go places during that time of the month because I was more likely to get sick for no apparent reason during that time. I knew there was a bigger risk then, but I wasn't sure why. I also knew that my swelling always got worse around my period and I watched as every month I would shrink more right after my period ended. There were signs in my life as well as from my body. Every time there was a family event or somewhere I *had* to go, it always seemed to be when I had my period. That was always when I felt the worst physically and with the anxiety. I used to say to Charlie all the time, why do I always have my period when I'm supposed to go somewhere?! Because I believe that there are no coincidences, I believed that there was a reason that this kept happening. We just didn't know what the reason was. Even my one kitty Gracie was a sign. When we first got her she was the cutest little thing ever. After we had her fixed, she blew up and got huge. She was not only overweight without eating any more than any of my other kitties did, she had dry skin under her fur, and problems with her intestines where she could only eat certain kinds of kitty food without getting sick. Every time someone would make a comment about Gracie having gotten so big I would tell them to leave her alone. It wasn't *her* fault. It was hormones. It didn't happen until after we had gotten her fixed. (I knew she wasn't supposed to be a big cat because she had little paws. Cats that are supposed to be big usually have bigger paws.) So there I was constantly saying "it was hormones" about Grace and ignoring the message that there may be a connection for myself. Often we get signs and messages from our pets. It happened for me on several occasions and this was just one of them.

Anyway, as I read more about female hormones I was shocked to learn all that they do in the body. I had always thought that female hormones did female "stuff" in the body. I didn't realize that they did SO MUCH more than that. I didn't realize that there were estrogen/progesterone receptors in the bladder, the vaginal tissues, and all over the body. I didn't realize that female hormones, when they were out of balance, could cause so many symptoms that had nothing to do with the female organs and menstrual cycle. And I'm sure I must have learned it at some point in biology class, but I didn't even remember that men had female hormones too! Now that I understand more what these hormones actually do, I can see why men need them even though they don't have female organs. Now I can understand why an imbalance between progesterone and the estrogens could be the cause of symptoms we would not normally associate with "female hormones".

But when I was sick with my bladder raw and bleeding, if someone would have told me that "it was hormones" I would have not only been insulted (I don't know...it's just not what any woman wants to hear I guess), I would have thought that they didn't know what they were talking about. IC is much more complicated than "just hormones" for many of us. And although I knew that IC (and a toxic body) had messed up my hormones, I didn't think they were the reason I had IC or any of my IC related symptoms. However, I did get horrible cramps, heavy periods, and breast tenderness with my IC and *that*, of course, I attributed to female hormones. But from what I was learning, I began to realize that the hormone connection with IC goes much deeper than that.

Hormones, in general, are regulators of body processes. They tell the cells, organs, and body systems what to do. The main role of the class of hormones called the estrogens is the stimulation of cell growth. Whether the estrogens are produced in the body (in the ovaries or in smaller amounts by the adrenal glands and body fat) or whether they are produced outside the body from birth control pills, HRT (hormone replacement therapy), or toxic chemicals in our food or environment (typically referred to as xenoestrogens), they all have this growth stimulating affect on cells. Among many other things, progesterone, in proper balance with the estrogens, keeps tissue growth in check. Too much estrogen (with not enough progesterone for balance) can cause out of control tissue growth that can lead to fibroid tumors, excess menstrual lining (resulting in heavy periods), breast or uterine cancer. Too much estrogen can lead to many other symptoms as well including water retention/edema, anxiety, abdominal bloating, insomnia, ovarian cysts, night sweats, craving for sweets, depression, tender and/or swollen breasts, fibrocystic breast disease, fatigue or lack of energy, low thyroid (cold hands and feet), multiple allergies, changes in menstrual cycle, headaches, bone loss, and heart palpitations. In fact, without enough progesterone to counteract the effects of excess estrogens, it can affect all the tissues in the body, including the breasts, vagina, bones, blood vessels, skin, gastrointestinal tract, and urinary tract.

As I was reading about all of this, I couldn't believe all the similarities between Estrogen Dominance and my remaining symptoms. I felt sure that this was an answer for me. I didn't have all the symptoms of Estrogen Dominance, but I did have several. I certainly had the edema, abdominal bloating, skin problems, and anxiety. And I knew that I had even more of the symptoms of Estrogen Dominance when I was sick with IC (e.g., hypothyroidism, cold hands and feet, heavy periods, tender/swollen breasts, multiple allergies, night sweats, headaches, heart palpitations, and trouble sleeping). I also knew, from talking with thousands of IC patients over the years, that I wasn't the only one to have these other symptoms come with their IC.

Looking more closely at the role of progesterone I began to notice even more connections with IC. Progesterone does many other things in the body besides keeping tissue growth in check. It is a natural diuretic, a natural anti-depressant, a natural blood vessel relaxor, and a natural blood sugar stabilizer. Also very important is the fact that progesterone is a precursor to not only testosterone and the estrogens, but also to the cortical steroids produced in the adrenal glands, which help prevent inflammation and block the histamine response to allergens. Many IC patients have multiple allergies and many have fibromyalgia with joint pain. Of course we all have inflammation since IC, by its medical definition, is the inflammation of the bladder wall. Adequate levels of progesterone are necessary for proper thyroid hormone function. Many IC patients also have thyroid problems (most common is hypothyroidism) and I believe that many, though they may not realize it, also have adrenal exhaustion (especially those with more severe cases of IC).

113

Progesterone, named for its tremendous role in pregnancy (i.e., pro-gestation), increases dramatically during pregnancy. It is literally a pro-life hormone. The health and growth of the fetus is dependant upon it. If excess estrogens were playing a role in IC for some people (which I now believe to be the case) it would explain why many IC patients go into remission during pregnancy. The increase in progesterone levels counteracts the excess estrogens and therefore reduces or eliminates symptoms. Some people even remain in remission following pregnancy. It's as if the huge surge in progesterone during the pregnancy has jolted their body back into balance. Other people experience the end of remission (or the onset of their first IC symptoms) once they deliver the baby when their progesterone level drops down again, much in the same way that some IC patients notice their IC symptoms beginning or getting worse immediately following a hysterectomy. Even mainstream medicine recognizes that many women, immediately following their hysterectomy, become allergic to all kinds of things that they weren't previously allergic to. Many believe that this is due to the sharp decline in progesterone (as it is primarily manufactured in the ovaries).

Obviously hysterectomies are not the only cause of low progesterone. There are several ways our hormones can get out of balance. Emotional and/or physical stress, chronic illness, heavy metal poisoning, a toxic colon and toxic body, infection, antibiotics and other pharmaceutical medications, and a B vitamin deficiency can all lead to hormonal imbalances. With IC, I believe many of us have several of these causes. Actually, by the time I got IC, I believe I had *all* of them.

Synthetic hormones like birth control pills, HRT, or fertility drugs can also cause our hormones to get out of balance. Birth control pills, for example, suppress ovulation and prevent a normal monthly surge of natural progesterone. Even though for some people, birth control pills help with PMS symptoms, cramps, and other menstrual difficulties, over time they can increase estrogen dominance. There are risks and side effects to synthetic hormones that they are only recently discovering. (In fact, I don't believe it was a coincidence that as I worked on this section of the book a Special News Report came on the television about how the FDA called a halt to the HRT study due to an increased risk of stroke, heart attack, breast cancer, and colon cancer.) Aside from synthetic hormones, there are so many other xenoestrogens we absorb from the chemicals in our environment, the antibiotics and hormones in meat and dairy products, the various over the counter and pharmaceutical medications we take, as well as all the other synthetic ingredients in our foods, that it is causing Estrogen Dominance to become much more prevalent.

Even aging can lead to hormonal imbalances. It is known that around age 35 a normal healthy woman's progesterone level usually drops. I thought it was interesting that I turned 35 the summer before my anxiety symptom began. I also thought it was interesting that when my IC was most severe and I had lost tons of weight because of it, that I missed at least 4 periods in a row. A lack of menstruation, as well as anovulatory cycles (meaning we are not actually ovulating even though we still get our period), both fail to produce the normal surge in progesterone by the ovaries.

I look back and realize that I most certainly had an imbalance in my hormones when I first got IC and even before I had IC. I believe that my hormones started getting out of balance back when I was in college when I was put on birth control pills for the first time. (Birth control pills basically stop you from ovulating so that you don't get pregnant and therefore also stop the normal surge of progesterone needed for a healthy hormonal balance.) I got off of them because I didn't like how I felt on them and that was when I got the first cyst on my ovary. I was 21 years old. Back then I had surgery and was better in two weeks. But then the doctor put me back on the pill telling me that it would help prevent any more cysts from coming. I listened for another year or two until they made me feel bad enough to get off them again. I feel sure that the birth control pills, which, by the way, I took at the same time in my life that I was hit in the face with the baseball bat, had something to do with my getting ovarian cysts and eventually getting IC. This was also the same time in my life that I started getting cramps and PMS symptoms, the same time that I started noticing that I had to go to the bathroom more often, the same time that I started getting sick more easily and the same time that I got my very first yeast infection. I can see now how my hormones were gradually getting more and more out of balance and that I was getting symptoms of Estrogen Dominance (or low progesterone) even back then.

But were my hormones the cause of my IC? Well...I don't think they were "the" cause, but I can tell you for certain that they were part of it. Actually, the more I learned and experienced these past 8 months, the more I realized that *it's all connected.*

"...*no* part of the body lives apart from the rest."
– Deepak Chopra (*Perfect Health*)

Chapter 9

It's All Connected

As I continued to read and learn more about Estrogen Dominance, I was given even more signs from the Universe as confirmation that I was on the right track. I spoke to my mom about it and she had just "coincidentally" received, that very week, a newsletter from Dr. Susan Lark regarding Estrogen Dominance and the role of progesterone in the body. I spoke to a friend of mine on the phone who was actually on a trip to California at the time where she just happen to meet a guy who was selling natural progesterone cream. Never before this had I even ever heard of Estrogen Dominance or natural progesterone cream and here it had come up in two conversations in less than a week. And then to top it all off, one week after reading all about what female hormones do in the body, I woke up with a pain on my left side. It was the first time I felt pain in over two years (except for occasional bad cramps with my cycle), and then I remembered. I remembered that I had felt that same exact kind of pain before, in that same exact location. It was at the start of my whole IC nightmare. This was the pain of an ovarian cyst. For me, it was what started the whole IC "thing" to begin with. That's when I realized I had gone full circle. Here I was, for the most part, completely better physically and now I had that pain back that started the whole thing to begin with! Thankfully, by the time I felt that pain on my left side, I had already read enough about hormone imbalances to learn that natural progesterone cream has been shown to reduce, shrink, and rid the body of ovarian cysts.

At first I got upset when I realized that if I had only known then what I know now, I would have used natural progesterone cream eight years ago to shrink my cysts instead of having surgery and most likely I would not have gotten IC at all. But then I remembered that everything happens for a reason. I knew I was supposed to get IC and write these books. I was supposed to try and help other people out of their IC nightmare. Everything happened just as it was supposed to.

So now I understood the rest of what I was meant to put in this book. Now I understood why I had those remaining symptoms. I was supposed to learn about this hormone connection with IC and share it with you. I never would have learned about it had I not had the anxiety symptom. And the more I learned about it (and the more I talked to other IC patients about it these past 8 months), the more I believed it to be a huge connection for many (but of course not all) people with IC.

Initially, some IC patients might discount the low progesterone theory for themselves for a couple of reasons. One reason is that many of us notice that our symptoms worsen from mid-cycle (ovulation) through the start of our menstrual cycle. This is the time that the body is supposed to have the most progesterone. So adding more progesterone seems to be the wrong thing to do. It seems like it would increase our symptoms even more. But actually, just because the body is *supposed* to have more progesterone during that time, doesn't mean that we actually have it. For me, that was the problem, that's what was causing my symptoms. The fact that during the time my body needed progesterone the most (or was supposed to have an increased supply), I barely had any (or at least not enough). The second reason that some IC patients may not think estrogen dominance or low progesterone is a problem for them is because they go to their doctor and have a hormone test done and it comes back looking like they are fine. The problem here is that in the past ten years or so they have found that blood tests do not accurately portray the hormone levels in our body. The good news is that saliva testing does. Not only is it painless and less expensive, but it also more accurately portrays our hormone levels than blood tests do. Blood tests only show the protein bound hormones, where saliva shows the biologically active hormones available to our tissues. Unfortunately medical doctors are still a little behind in terms of switching over to the saliva hormone tests (even though they've been the standard used by the World Health Organization for over 5 years), so we need to either go to a holistic/alternative/naturopath type doctor or we can go the cheaper route and go directly through a lab to be tested. Anyway, that's what I did. I sent a saliva sample to a lab that specializes in saliva hormone testing and my results confirmed what I knew would be the case. I had very low levels of progesterone and the ratio or the balance between estrogen and progesterone, which is what is most important, was way below normal.

So there it was, another physical cause of my anxiety symptom and quite possibly the reason for all of my remaining symptoms. And the best thing about it was that the solution, get this, is a CREAM! You put it on like you would lotion! I could barely believe it! After all the things I had to do to get better, giving up great food, sex, going places, etc., and all the stuff I had to do, quitting smoking, getting my fillings replaced, cleansing yeast and dealing with die-off symptoms, drinking icky tasting herbs, swimming when I was swollen, etc. to find out that all I had to do was use a natural progesterone cream, I was ecstatic.

The connections on paper were one thing, but what really blew me away were the connections I saw and felt in my own body as I started using the natural progesterone cream. I tried not to freak out as all kinds of symptoms I had with my IC, symptoms I hadn't had for at least 2-3 years, things I never would have thought had anything at all to do with my hormones, started to return. Not to the degree I had them back then, but certainly enough for me to recognize them. Thank God, they didn't last too long. Some things came back for a week or two, others for a day. Some things came back during the time of the month that I was not using the progesterone cream, and then when I would start using it again, they would go away immediately. It was as if these symptoms were coming back up to be healed completely. I stopped worrying and started to realize that they were just more signs. More signs for me to know and understand that nearly all of the symptoms I had with my IC, though all of them were most certainly caused by *multiple* physical reasons, did in fact have some connection to low levels of progesterone.

As I was saying, many of my symptoms came back temporarily when I began using the natural progesterone. For example, with my IC came severe joint pain, especially in my knees. This symptom had been gone for well over two years by the time I started on the progesterone. But for the first several months on the natural progesterone cream, each month, at the time I would stop using the cream, my knees would kill in just the same way they used to, until I would get back on the cream and it would go right away. Once I noticed this connection between my joint pain and my hormones I found it interesting (now that I know that antibiotics can mess up your hormones) that my joint pain came immediately after taking a course of strong antibiotics. Another connection I noticed as I used the cream was that my gums began to bother me again in much the same way as my knees where I had symptoms off the cream, but none while I was on it. I should have guessed that my teeth and gums problems might be related to my hormones because I did notice that each month at the time of my cycle my teeth and gums would bother me way more than they did during the rest of the month. Yet another sign that it took time to understand. But now I understand another reason why IC patients can be prone to teeth and gum problems whether they have metal in their mouth or not. And why those of us who do have mercury fillings in our mouths tend to have more sensitivity to them those who don't have IC. I now believe that all of the mucous membranes in the body are affected by excess estrogen, including the mouth, the vagina, the intestines, and the bladder. That's how it was for me.

I also found a relationship between low progesterone and my intestines. Once I began using the cream I started to be able to get nervous without it making me physically sick in my intestines. The IBS-like symptoms of extreme diarrhea with painful cramps and the nausea

122

were occurring much less often. Something else that returned temporarily for me while I was on the progesterone cream was a very acid stomach and symptoms of acid reflux. You know that feeling of burning in the chest and upper stomach, especially when you lay down to go to sleep at night? I had that in a horrible way with my IC and since I had gotten better it was gone. But with the progesterone cream, it came back for a very short time (thank God!) and now of course it's gone again. I believe that excess estrogens can contribute to an acid body. Some other connections I found between my symptoms and having low progesterone had to do with bloating, edema, fibromyalgia, carpal tunnel, bloody noses, and headaches. But that's not all. Something else completely unexpected happened while I was on the natural progesterone cream. My bladder went to a whole new level of wellness. I mean, I had been better bladder-wise for quite some time (at least 2-3 years), but this was even better. It was like my bladder got even stronger. I could wait even longer between bathroom trips. Now I feel even more normal bladder-wise than I even did before!

Another exciting connection I found was with vulvodynia. Vulvodynia, at least for me was very much related to low progesterone and a lack of B vitamins. It was the combination of those two factors that, for the most part, resulted in vulvodynia symptoms. I had finally understood why last year when I overdid it on the B vitamins, I ended up with that horrible VV reaction. I now believe there is a huge connection between our body's ability to tolerate B vitamins and having excess estrogens in our system. It's as if, without enough progesterone, the B vitamins burn the mucous membranes in the bladder, vaginal tissues, and probably elsewhere. Or maybe the B's simply cause a cleanse and the toxins that are released are burning the tissues. I'm not sure, but I can tell you that since using the natural progesterone cream I haven't had a single hint of vulvodynia again, to the point where I am now back on B vitamins again with no problems.

This was not the first time B vitamins played a role in my symptoms. As you know, I believe there to be a huge connection between B vitamin deficiency and sensitivity, IC, and stress. And now I was amazed as I realized that the stress connection with IC that I had written about in *Along the Healing Path* had one more important component...the balance between progesterone and the estrogens. Excess estrogens greatly impact our body's ability to handle stress for many reasons. Too much estrogen compared to progesterone can stimulate the nervous system too much and can create anxiety and insomnia. Excess estrogens affect the neurotransmitters in the brain such as epinephrine, which at high levels causes anxiety. Stress causes high levels of cortisol to be produced by the adrenals and cortisol blocks progesterone from attaching to receptor sites. Even normal progesterone production by healthy ovaries might not be enough to overcome the blockade from high cortisol levels. Also, as mentioned, progesterone is a precursor to the other hormones produced in the adrenal glands that help our body deal with stress. Therefore, in times of stress, more progesterone may be needed, and often that is when we have an even lower supply and/or it is being blocked by cortisol. Lower levels of progesterone (or excess estrogens) therefore lower our resistance to the effects of stress. Not only does a B vitamin deficiency (which I believe most IC patients have) cause too much estrogen in the body, too much estrogen depletes the body of B vitamins, magnesium, and zinc. In order for our body to handle stress, whether physical or emotional, our adrenal glands need not only enough vitamin C and B vitamins, but also they need enough progesterone! It was all connected!

And as if that wasn't enough, I almost fell out of my chair when I read that estrogens, in excess, actually become toxic to the body. Estrogen Dominance is another source of toxicity to the body! If I had known about all of this when I wrote *Along the Healing Path* I would have included Estrogen Dominance as another possible internal source of toxicity. I was beginning to see why some IC patients I spoke with who didn't have any obvious sources of toxicity were still exhibiting symptoms of someone with a toxic body. Or why some people who had removed all sources of toxicity and cleansed (like I had) still seemed to remain toxic. And oh my God! It's why maybe even I still remained toxic...?

I started to realize that I did still have symptoms of toxicity. How did I not see this before?! I guess I had thought that because I had removed all the sources of toxicity that I could think of and because I had cleansed so much while I was healing from IC that I simply couldn't be toxic anymore. And I was doing so much better in so many ways that I guess I wasn't even considering toxicity to be part of the problem anymore. I didn't realize that I still had an internal source of toxicity. I never would have imagined that my hormones could be causing me to remain toxic. And I did wonder if maybe I hadn't cleansed enough after having my fillings replaced. Of that, I couldn't be sure. However, I did know that I still had a swollen gland under my left arm that never went down all the way. And I did know that I was still breaking out on my skin (like I did when I was cleansing) and it wasn't just an acne type of breakout, it was like little blisters. And of course I knew that I still had swelling. Now that I think about it, I also realized that my swelling always got worse at certain times (aside from during the second half of my cycle), like after a hot shower or bath, after working out or swimming, after standing for too long or wearing tight clothes, after eating, and at night. These are all times when toxins are more active. And in terms of my intestines, even though it was occurring less often, I was still getting those poison rush feelings (as I always used to call them) with the IBS-like symptoms. And I was still "going far away in my head" during those times, just like I used to do when I was really sick. Oh my God! And that's really what I was still so afraid of! That was the psychological basis of my anxiety about going places. I was afraid because I never knew when I was going to get those poison rush feelings and the "going far away in my head" feelings and then of course needing to be in the bathroom immediately. On a psychological level, that's really what was making me so nervous about going places. Just because it wasn't AS BAD as it was when I was really sick with IC and just because my bladder was better, didn't mean that I wasn't still toxic. I felt pretty stupid when I realized that *all this time* the answers were staring me right in the face. The answers were in my symptoms, but I had lost perspective. I hadn't been listening to my body. I was thinking one certain way about my symptoms and I had stopped listening to what my symptoms were telling me.

When I was sick with IC, I was aware that my body was toxic and out of balance in many ways. Actually, I believe that is the case for many people with IC, especially those who also have some of the other fairly common IC related illnesses such as Fibromyalgia, IBS, Vulvodynia, multiple chemical sensitivity, etc. When you have IC, especially a more severe case, it is more than likely that you are out of balance in more than just one way. Many of us have an acid/alkaline imbalance where are bodies are too acidic. Many of us also have a yeast imbalance where there are not enough good bacteria to balance out the yeast in the intestines. Some people also have a blood sugar imbalance, a thyroid hormone imbalance, and/or a sodium/potassium imbalance. And many of us, I now believe, also have an imbalance of our female hormones. And an imbalance in our female hormones, I discovered, could also be affecting the balance of *all the other things* IC patients are often out of balance in! For me, it was definitely all connected. In fact, I could barely believe it. Everything I had written about in my first two books about how IC patients have a toxic body, about the connection between stress and IC, the connection between allergies and IC, the connection between our thyroid and IC, and the connection between yeast and IC, all of these connections were also connected (in part) to the hormone connection with IC.

There are a lot of connections with IC. Hormones are only part of the picture. In fact, one day a few months ago as I was thinking about how everything was connected and how there were multiple causes to my IC (and IC related symptoms), I sat down and drew the following diagram of my IC.

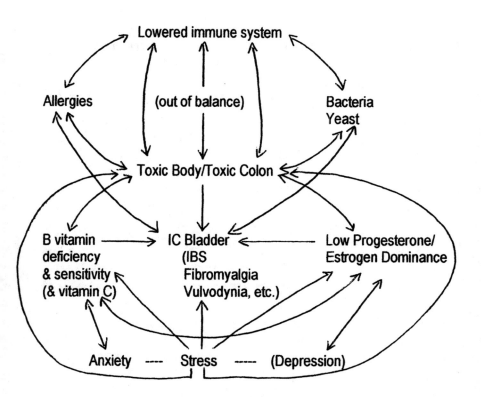

Though we all have different external and internal sources of toxicity and none of us are toxic to the same degree, toxicity is, in my opinion, a definite common trait among IC patients. The more severe the IC, the more toxic the body is likely to be and the more likely the person will have multiple other IC related symptoms and illnesses. Toxicity in the body, whether due to a toxic colon, sluggish lymph glands, and/or a constant barrage of internal and external sources of toxicity, lowers or weakens the immune system making a person more susceptible to infection of all kinds. Allergies, yeast overgrowth, excess estrogens and stress are all sources of toxicity to the body. There are other possible sources of toxicity as well, including (but not limited to) cigarette smoking, mercury amalgam fillings, constipation, pharmaceutical medications, synthetic/chemical ingredients in foods, and chemicals in the environment. Bacteria, yeast and viruses all thrive in a toxic environment. With infection often come antibiotics and/or antifungals, which suppress the immune system further and throw the hormones out of balance. Of course antibiotics also affect the balance of intestinal flora promoting yeast infections. Yeast releases toxins into the body further increasing toxicity. Antibiotics, like many pharmaceutical medications can cause constipation, which also adds to toxicity. Constipation can actually prevent the liver from filtering unwanted estrogens. When the colon and body are toxic and the liver is unable to properly regulate hormone balance, excess estrogens can build up in the body. Another cause of excess estrogens in the body is a lack of B vitamins because B vitamins help the liver convert excess estrogens to a harmless form. IC patients can have all of these reasons and more to have excess estrogens. Excess estrogens also become toxic to the body. With a lowered immune system, out of balance hormones, and a toxic colon/body we are more prone to allergies and sensitivities. The allergens further weaken our immune system and cause us to become even more toxic. With our bodies on toxic overload, they are just naturally trying to release as many toxins as possible and therefore much stress is put onto our eliminative organs (e.g., the bladder, intestines, and skin) as well as the lymph glands, liver, and kidneys that filter and help rid the body of waste. A toxic body causes an imbalance in our hormones and in turn, an imbalance in our hormones causes more toxicity in the body. Excess estrogens cause the body to become more toxic and less able to tolerate the B vitamins (and vitamin C) that it so desperately needs. The body needs the B's to not only handle stress, but also to help it eliminate some of the toxicity. (B vitamins help release toxins from the body.) Having excess estrogens and a B vitamin deficiency lowers our ability to deal with stress and can cause emotional symptoms of depression and/or anxiety. (I included depression in parenthesis in my diagram because, even though I didn't have that symptom, I know a lot of people experience depression with their IC.) Feeling anxiety and feeling depressed then puts further strain on our immune system thus adding even more stress on the body. The more stress on the body, the longer we stay out of balance hormone-wise and deficient in the vitamins and minerals we need, the more toxic and sick we get.

It becomes a cycle, a cycle where everything is connected. I believe that for many of us it is a combination of these factors that lead to IC *and* keep us sick with IC. It is interesting to note when looking at the diagram that allergies, bacteria, yeast, B vitamins (or vitamin C), stress and excess estrogens can ALL (both individually and collectively) cause IC symptoms.

There are many pieces of the puzzle and of course they are going to be a little different for each person. Naturally not everyone will have all of the same factors that I did or to the same degree. The main thing to recognize, in my opinion, is that it is all connected. Each thing affects the other. Our bladder does not exist separate from our body. What is going on in the rest of our body can, and often does, have an affect on our bladder. What we do to our body, what we put into it, and what we put it through, can, and often does, have an affect on our bladder. Stress on the body (in any form) makes everything worse.

Stress is almost an automatic if you have IC. I think for many people it is very stressful just trying to get diagnosed. For some people it takes several years (and several doctors) which is a long time to deal with physical symptoms that no one believes are real. It is very stressful and emotionally painful to not be believed when you're physically sick. Even once we get diagnosed, there are often still people who don't believe IC is real and who still treat us as if we should be able to do everything that we used to do (and everything that they want us to do). It's very stressful on our body to continue to do things that physically we are not up to. It is also very stressful thinking that we might be in pain and suffering this way for the rest of our life. Not to mention that it is stressful on the body just being sick to begin with. The extra stress from having IC (aside from the normal stressors in our lives) also messes up our hormones and depletes our body of vital nutrients.

Once we finally get diagnosed with IC we are often subjected to even more things that cause an imbalance in our hormones and even further deplete our body of vital nutrients. First there are the "normal" medications for IC, the tricyclic anti-depressants, the Pyridium, the pain medication, the anti-spasmodic medication, the bladder coating drugs, that all further deplete the body of vitamins, add more toxicity, and further mess up hormone balance. And then if you get an infection while you have IC or decide to take long-term antibiotics to fight the IC, the antibiotics also mess up your hormone balance even further and suppress your immune system even more. And if your hormones are already out of balance and you already have multiple allergies, a toxic body, and a weakened immune system, (which I believe many with IC have) and then you are subjected to a latex catheter or dye from an IVP, for example, you might have a reaction from that where a "normal" person might not. It can become a cycle where the things that we try to do or take to help us get better, can end up making us even worse.

But it works the other way around as well. Sometimes when we address one of the causes, it will help with another cause. For example, cleansing your colon of yeast (if yeast is a factor for you) will help reduce toxicity in your body making you less susceptible to allergies and infections. Reducing stress will help conserve the supply of available vitamins, minerals, and hormones needed for healing. Reducing the toxins that enter the body or that the body is exposed to will aid the body in healing itself in numerous ways. Making the body less toxic will automatically boost the immune system, reduce the risk of infections of all kinds, and help the body to not be so sensitive. These are some of the things that I did to heal my bladder and body. Healing from IC, for me, was about understanding and addressing all of those connections. It was about treating my whole body, not just my bladder. It was about determining what was out of balance and finding a way to get it back into balance. And not just in my body, but in my life as well. Just as our bladder does not exist separate from our body, our body does not exist separate from our mind and our spirit. It is all connected.

"Only when you say, "I did this" can you find
the power to change it."
- *Conversations with God, book 1*

Chapter 10

◆

Why me?

Finally, I am listening to my body again. And finally I am realizing what it is that I was so afraid of. I was afraid because I didn't understand what was going on inside my body. I was afraid because I had no control over what was happening. I was afraid because I never knew *when* it was going to happen. And I was afraid because at those times, I felt like NO ONE could help me. It's exactly like when I had IC. The more mystery there was about what was going on inside my body, the more afraid I became. The longer it took me to get diagnosed, the more doctors who told me that it was "in my head" when I *knew* it wasn't, the more stressed out and afraid I became. And even once I was diagnosed and found out that the medical community didn't really have any answers for me, the mysteries continued. And so did the stress and the fear. And then I was trying to heal myself with alternatives and I was basically on my own in that regard. This of course added even more stress and more mystery. Like with many things in life, it's the "not knowing" that makes it all the more scary. Just like with IC, I felt no control over what was happening to my body. Just like with my IC, I felt there was no one who could help me. And I felt extremely alone in what I was going through because of it.

But now, now that I feel like I understand more of what was going on inside my body, now that I understand what I have to do to get better and what was happening when I was feeling sick and panicky, I feel like *now* I can get better. *Now* I don't have to be so afraid anymore. It's funny because that's one thing I was trying to give others through my first two books. I was hoping to offer IC patients more understanding of their IC and other IC related symptoms so that they wouldn't be so afraid. And why? Because I knew *exactly* what it was like to be that afraid, to feel that my body was falling apart and that no one could help me. And I couldn't bare the thought that so many other people were out there, alone in their bathrooms, alone in their bodies, feeling that same pain and that same fear. It's unbelievably scary (especially if you have a more severe case) and I don't think many people really understand that part of having IC. (I say that like there are parts they do understand.)

Now I believe I understand how my anxiety/panicky feelings came about, both on a physical and a psychological level, as well as how they were related to my IC. Now I can see why it felt like my intellect and body weren't connected and why all the positive self-talk and intellectual reasoning wasn't helping me with the anxiety/panicky feelings. It was because they were being caused by something physical.

On a physical level, panic and anxiety are the result of a tired, overworked nervous system. When our body perceives a danger of any kind, the brain sends a signal to the pituitary gland, which then sends a signal to the adrenal glands, which then release adrenaline (epinephrine) and other chemicals and hormones to help the body to deal with the danger. This is what is called the "fight or flight mode". As I mentioned earlier in the book, this is where I lived the whole time I was sick. I was constantly in that fight or flight mode. Though for me it was mostly because of having IC, there are many things that can cause that kind of high alert status in the body. Feelings such as anger, sorrow, anxiety, and worry, as well as strenuous exercise, caffeine, sugar, being in a hurry all the time, multi-tasking (i.e., doing a lot of things at one time), and constantly trying to please other people. All of these things can cause the body to be in this high stress mode. Our nervous system, like our body, needs balance. If we are bothered by something 8 hours a day, then we need an equal 8 hours a day of rest to allow our nervous system to rejuvenate. The more the balance shifts toward too much stress with not enough rest, the more overtired the nervous system will become. Often we don't listen to our body's signals telling us to rest. Many people cover up the small symptoms like a headache or a cold, for example, with an aspirin or a cold medicine, and then go on, instead of resting. Or maybe they feel stressed out so maybe they smoke a cigarette or have a drink or something, and again, they go on, instead of resting. And eventually they get sick with something more than just a little headache or cold. Over time, the balance between stress and time to rest is so thrown off that they can get sick with more serious things. Things like IC, for example.

Before I got IC, several very stressful things occurred in my life. I would say that I was definitely on overload. I was not getting enough rest, or any type of break, from the stress. And then once I got sick with IC, my balance between stress and rest was *way* off. Every minute of the day and most of the night, I was on high alert status. The stress was not only from external stressors anymore, but also from within me from my mysterious physical symptoms. Of course I also had strong emotions such as fear and worry about these mysterious symptoms. My body needed time to rest and recover and so did my nervous system. But there was no time for that. I had to read and research and figure out how to get better. I had to deal with horribly painful symptoms while at the same time dealing with people not believing that I was really sick. I had to deal with these symptoms without having anyone who I could really count on to understand what was going on inside my body enough to be able to help me. I had to continue trying to go places and do things that were "expected" of me. At least I felt like I had to. And even as I was getting better physically, I ended up writing a book, and then another. I was spending most all of my time trying to help other IC patients. I never allowed my body and nervous system enough time to rest and fully recover. And then, once my symptoms became mysterious to me again, the "danger" that my body perceived was again, coming from inside of me. Just like with IC, I had no way of getting away from it. This made it very tough to relax and get the rest I so desperately needed. Not only did the constant releasing of adrenaline make me more sensitive and stressed, when you have IC (and all that goes with it) it makes it difficult to go places and do things, which adds even more fuel to the "fear cycle". I think this must happen to a lot of IC patients. For me, even once I was so much better, due to the nature of my remaining symptoms and the fact that they could happen at any time, I became afraid to go places and do things, which then, of course, made things even worse. The fear of getting sick when I went somewhere would trigger my nervous system to respond and release adrenaline, which would then make me physically sick. It became a cycle that I didn't know how to break.

I had an exhausted nervous system that I never really gave a chance to recover. I had mysterious symptoms that contained scary components, plus the risk of embarrassment, so naturally I became psychologically nervous, which would then cause more symptoms by further stressing my nervous system (and immune system), depleting my body of B vitamins (as well as other nutrients) AND progesterone, thus making me more toxic, which is what was causing my symptoms to begin with! This is EXACTLY the same cycle that happens with IC that can make us sick and keep us sick.

Interestingly, what caused my remaining symptoms on a physical level were essentially the same factors involved in my getting IC to begin with. B vitamin deficiency, low progesterone/excess estrogens, a toxic body, an overworked nervous system and lymph system, and exhausted adrenal glands due to physical and emotional stress. Eventually, even more factors were involved in why I had the symptoms I had with my IC, including bacteria, yeast, and allergies. But the initial factors are the same. As I was writing this I just realized that I was still dealing with the bottom half of the diagram! I truly *had* gone full circle. I now believe that this is how the anxiety and IC are connected for me and probably for many people.

I realize now that I wasn't listening to my body a long time ago either. I had been gradually getting more and more out of balance, gradually getting more and more toxic, without really realizing it was happening. I had done things to my body that, at the time, I thought were no big deal. Things like taking birth control pills and antibiotics for example. We are told that they are basically "safe" and I doubt I was alone in thinking that they are no big deal. But what I've learned since having IC is that nothing is without risk. No synthetic medication, no synthetic hormone, no synthetic chemicals that we put into or expose our body to, are without risks. What I've learned is that just because something is "FDA approved" doesn't mean that it is automatically proven to be safe. It is nearly the opposite where something is considered safe until proven otherwise. And what I also learned is that it is pretty tough to prove it otherwise. I mean it took over 60 deaths to get a diabetes medication off the market last year. That's a lot of people that died before they figured it out. There are many medications that have been pulled off the shelf after the public has used them for years. But I wasn't thinking about that kind of thing years ago. I wasn't thinking about the billions of dollars involved in the sale of these drugs or the kickbacks and freebies that some doctors enjoy when they prescribe them. I just went along and trusted the doctor (as we are all told to do), never researching things for myself or even thinking too much about it. I wasn't thinking about my dental fillings either. I assumed that they were safe just because they've been used for years and so many people have them. If I hadn't been sick with IC I don't think I would have learned that mercury amalgam has been banned in several other countries or how there are countless studies out there that prove that mercury in the mouth or in the body is harmful. I probably wouldn't have even thought about how logically, it makes no sense whatsoever that it would be safe and perfectly okay to have a known poison in your mouth. But before I got sick, none of these things were even part of my thinking. I went along believing and trusting that the FDA, ADA, or whoever, wouldn't allow certain things if they weren't safe. But now I know better. And now I know that little by little, exposure to things like artificial sweeteners, mercury amalgam, synthetic hormones, and pharmaceutical medications, can really screw up your body. Especially when you add to it that you're not getting enough exercise, you're under a ton of stress, and you're not getting enough rest. And *especially* when you're deficient in the major nutrients your body needs to process all that poison and synthetic stuff.

It is interesting that there are now people like Dr. Christine Northrup author of *Women's Body, Women's Wisdom,* who recommend that a person should take B vitamins if they are going to take birth control pills (or any synthetic hormones) because they are known to deplete the body of B vitamins. But just as medical doctors often fail to tell their patients that taking acidophilus when you take antibiotics will help prevent yeast problems, I'm sure it is rare for medical doctors to tell their patients on HRT or birth control pills that they should take B vitamins to prevent other health problems. I know I certainly was never told either. I never realized I was causing a yeast imbalance when I took antibiotics (because they kill good bacteria along with the bad) or that antibiotics could even affect my hormones. And I never realized that birth control pills were depleting my body of B vitamins and causing a hormonal imbalance. All I thought was "oh isn't this nice that I know exactly when I'm going to get my period and that the flow is lighter" and I thought "oh isn't this nice if it helps with cramps and prevents cysts", "oh and by the way, now I don't have to worry about getting pregnant either". All of that is pretty tempting when you put on top of it "my doctor told me to" and "all my friends are taking them". These days they are promoting the pill as an acne fighter. There is even a new one out that is being advertised as helping with weight loss. All of this is extraordinarily tempting to teenagers and young women. Like so many before me (and so many still), I never thought about the fact that I was messing with nature or that it could affect me so much, especially because I had always been so healthy.

I didn't realize that years ago I had put into motion a cycle. A cycle of hormonal imbalance mixed together with a deficiency in the B vitamins and vitamin C, which would eventually spiral into a toxic body with a lowered immune system, infections, yeast overgrowth, allergies, and symptoms all over my body. Eventually there were extra stressors (i.e., the surgeries, my dad dying, getting divorced, changing jobs) that put me over the edge and into the fun filled abyss of IC. The synthetic hormones, the toxicity, the infection, the allergic reaction to the latex catheter, the yeast (and all the other sources of toxicity such as smoking, mercury amalgam, and stress), they all played a role in my IC. Stress reduced my body's ability to cleanse out the toxins and also added more toxicity. Stress, both emotional and physical, lowered my resistance, further depleted my body of B vitamins, suppressed my immune system, and threw my hormones even further out of balance. The more toxic I became, the more sensitive to everything I became, the more these allergens added physical stress to my body. I had poison coming from within me and from without. I had poison in my physical body and I even had poison in my emotions.

As the toxins were building up in my body and I was getting more and more out of balance, the negative and painful emotions I was feeling were also building up. I had tipped the scale in terms of how much emotional pain I was carrying. It wasn't as much that I was "holding on to it" as it was that I had gotten such a huge dose all at the same time. There was the emotional pain from the divorce and from the verbal abuse prior to the divorce, the huge emotional pain from missing my dad, and the anger at myself for not sticking up for myself sooner at my job and within my first marriage. I didn't realize the affect that all the stress of holding that much negative emotion was having on my physical body. I guess I just thought that I was mentally strong enough to handle it all. Now I can see that that has nothing to do with it. A body can only take so much. It wasn't my fault! I didn't do it on purpose. It was just a cycle that got out of control.

And this was why I got sick. This is why all of this happened to me. It wasn't that I was being "punished" by God and it wasn't just some horrible stroke of bad luck. I drew IC to me on every level, physically, emotionally, and spiritually, even though I didn't realize it when it was happening. As I said earlier, I got IC because I was out of balance in my body, in my emotions and in my life. In order to heal fully, I had to get back into balance in every way. I had to break the cycle.

Breaking the cycle takes understanding the causes and it takes time to address them all. Even though I knew that getting over my remaining symptoms would not happen overnight, naturally, I was still getting frustrated that it was taking so long. Even as I was rebalancing my hormones, I kept getting so upset. Every time I turned around there seemed to be something else right up ahead that I had to be nervous about. Well I didn't *have* to be nervous about it, but I would anyway because of what I was going through. Whether it was Charlie going out of town on business, a family event that I was supposed to go to, a haircut appointment, *anything*. Anything where I had to be somewhere at a certain time, go far away from my house, or if I had to be alone overnight without Charlie around, I would get worried that I might get sick. Certain things were going to come up regardless, but there were many things that I didn't really *have* to do; yet I was still trying to do them anyway. Things like meeting friends to go to a movie and out to dinner, going downtown to a baseball game, or going to the other side of town to my brothers house, they all made me completely stressed out because I didn't know if I would make it through the event without getting horribly scary sick. I kept saying to Charlie, "why does there always have to *be* something?" And of course I knew the answer. (It was kind of a dumb question really.) But my point was that I needed time to rest. Resting without worry and stress. Resting is what I knew that I needed, yet for some reason I was still not allowing it for myself.

Though I knew it was exhausting for me and I hated it so much every time it happened, I still didn't realize the magnitude of how much stressing out for each event that came up was affecting me. I didn't realize that it was actually helping to keep me sick. And then one day I finally got angry about it. I finally got angry with myself for making myself try and go to things that I knew, the day of them (and the night before) I was going to go through hell physically (and emotionally).

Ironically, the same emotion (anger) that helped to get me sick in the first place (on one level anyway) is the same emotion I needed to get better. I had to get angry enough with myself to get myself to stop doing what everyone was telling me to do (the baby steps), stop making myself go places that I was going to feel scared and stress out about, stop doing things and putting myself in horrible situations that were only making me feel worse. Oh my God! I just realized that this is EXACTLY the same thing I had to do to get better from IC. I had to stop listening to what other people were telling me to do and do what I felt was right for me. I had to stop doing things that other people wanted me to do when I didn't feel physically up to it or when I knew it would make me physically worse. I had to stop caring what they thought and concentrate on getting myself better. I had to start putting myself first for a change. I had to BE NICE TO MYSELF. Interestingly enough, all of these things I needed to do happened to be things that I wasn't too good at (and didn't do for myself) *before* I got sick. I've always been so lousy at being nice to myself that I actually had to get angry enough with myself to get myself to do it!

Anger, I've learned, doesn't always have to be negative. If anger at myself was what it was going to take for me to stop doing things that I wasn't ready to do and to start being nicer to myself, than so be it. I would embrace my anger and use it to empower and motivate me, just like I did after being diagnosed with IC. And just like with the IC, I had to get angry and decide that I was going to beat this thing. I had to choose to believe that I was going to get better. And I also had to let it be okay if I didn't. I had to let it be okay in terms of, if I was going to have this the rest of my life than there must be a higher reason for it and I was going to love and accept myself regardless. I had to allow myself the "luxury" of being afraid (and not going places because of being afraid) without totally hating myself for it. I had to stop blaming myself and thinking badly of myself for feeling this way. That's what I mean by I had to let it be okay. But I didn't have to accept it as my fate as if there was nothing I could do to at least *try* and change it. They say "God helps those who help themselves" and maybe that's what they mean by that. I was going to do whatever was humanly possible to figure this out. And I had to believe that I would because if I believed that I would, then I knew I would have a MUCH greater chance of doing so. And I had to have faith. Faith that everything is as it should be in every moment of time and faith that whatever I asked, God would answer. I had to have the kind of faith that I never used to have. I had to believe in miracles. And I did. I had seen nothing but continuous miracles occur in my life, especially since I started paying so much attention the past several years. So I did believe and I did have faith. I just had to remember that I did.

It's so funny and ironic to me that here I was writing a book about my awakening spiritually while I was healing from IC and then I come to realize that the spiritual reason/message behind one of my very last symptoms (the anxiety/panicky feelings) had to do with me not having enough faith. I didn't have enough faith that physically I was going to be okay; that *I am okay*. Believing that I wasn't okay, that something was wrong with me, was the core belief that, on one level, probably got me sick in the first place. I can see now that I believed, somewhere inside of me, and probably for most of my life, that there was something wrong with me or that I wasn't like everybody else. I knew that I wasn't perfect. And I guess that I thought I should be or at least that I wanted to be. I'm sure a lot of people grow up thinking, for whatever reason, that there's something wrong with them, that they're not like everybody else or that they're not good enough. When I was healing from IC, besides having to learn that "I count" and that my feelings matter, I also had to learn that I was good enough. I needed to learn that I didn't have to be perfect or even try to be; that I am okay JUST THE WAY I am. I needed to learn that there is nothing wrong with me. Realizing this and believing this was key for me. It's where it all started and it is where it will end.

Like many people with IC, I had to deal with the emotional pain of having people not care (or not believe) that I was physically sick. I remember wondering and asking Charlie if it was my fault that they didn't care. Was there something about me that I didn't deserve their concern or compassion? What was wrong with me that my own relatives didn't seem to care if I was sick in the hospital or suffering so much physically? What was wrong with me that people who supposedly cared about me, really didn't? *What was wrong with me?!* I finally had to learn that *there is nothing wrong with me!* It wasn't my fault that they didn't understand or seem to care. It wasn't about something being wrong with *me.* It was about what was going on in *their* lives and minds. It was about that they just didn't understand something like IC or how bad it could be. And some people, until something similar happens to them, will never even *try* to understand. I had to learn that it wasn't just me that this was happening to either. This happens to a lot of people with IC and other difficult to understand, invisible illnesses like IC. I had to learn that it wasn't all about me personally. And at the same time, looking at it from a different perspective, I also realized that they were just reflecting back to me how I felt about myself. I needed to change that primary belief that I had been carrying around with me most of my life in order to help change my reality. That primary belief that, on one level, probably helped draw an illness to me in the first place, that helped create, on a physical level, "something wrong with me". But primary beliefs that we carry through most of our lives are not so easy to change. So here I am, yet again, learning to accept myself for who I am, imperfections and all. Still, I am learning that "I am okay".

In terms of the anxiety, I again have to believe and affirm that there is nothing wrong with me. I have to say it out loud and write it down. "I no longer have IC and I am not ultra sensitive anymore. If something were to go wrong with me physically, someone could actually help me without totally hurting me in the process. I am okay. I am more than okay. I am healthy and strong. There is nothing wrong with me!" *Believing* all of this is what I need to do now. Ironically, *believing* that I would get well is what really got me well…it was the force driving me toward wellness, the force driving me toward the answers I needed to get well…and yet, here I am now, needing to believe that I actually AM well. Hilarious.

I realized that the past year and a half I have been telling other people and myself that "I can't", that "I'm too scared and I can't do it." And though it was true at the time (and in reality still is as I'm writing this) I also realize that I'm making it even MORE true by saying it all the time. I am re-creating it in the future by sending those thoughts out into the universe. As much as I feel like I've been trying to pay attention to this whole mind/body/spirit connection "thing", here again I realize, that I wasn't paying attention. I learned again that we have to watch what we tell ourselves about ourselves. We have to watch how we describe our body, our self, and our life. If we don't want to create it or re-create it, we have to stop talking like it is so. For example, while I was sick and my IBS was still severe, I kept on saying over and over again that I was scared of "going far away". And now, here I am, scared of going *places* far away. From one perspective I helped create this reality by saying it over and over again. (It's amazing the symbolism and the connections when you start to notice them.)

I've learned again how important it is to focus my thoughts on what I want to create rather than on what appears to be the reality in front of my face. But it's not easy. It definitely takes practice. Even as I address the physical aspects of my anxiety/fear, I still also realize that another way for me to stop experiencing it is to stop talking about it, thinking about it and writing about it. (Geez…I better hurry up and finish this book!)

So I started to change my thinking about it and began thinking instead about how brave I have been through this whole IC nightmare. Instead of focusing on how afraid I had become, I started to acknowledge that it took courage for me to get this far and I started cutting myself some slack. I started to see that it took a lot of courage for me to go to all the places I had gone when my IC was severe and maybe even more so since the anxiety/panicky feelings started. Why hadn't I looked at it like this before? I started to write and say affirmations to help me heal, just as I had done with all of my other IC and IC related symptoms. I wrote down affirmations like "I am brave. I am calm and relaxed no matter what the circumstances. I am safe and healthy. I see myself going places, feeling calm, and enjoying myself." Even though I had to treat the anxiety on a physical level, the affirmations were to help further create this in my reality. Actually, I said the affirmations before figuring out the final answer to the anxiety on a physical level. Sometimes the mind and thoughts must change before it can manifest into the physical.

I began to focus my thoughts on being the way I wanted myself to be. I pictured myself going places and doing things with confidence and calmness. I imagined myself feeling inside that sense of peace that I used to feel. I remembered what it was like to feel inner strength and also physical strength in my body. Strength where I wouldn't worry about what was coming up ahead because I knew for certain that I could deal with it no matter what it was. And I imagined myself feeling that way again. I prayed to God and thanked Him for healing me the rest of the way, for being there for me the entire time I had IC even when I had thought He wasn't listening. Because now I know He was (and is) always listening…*and answering*. I just hadn't understood how before. I thanked God for my new confidence and inner strength even before I noticed the change in me physically. And I waited for the signs, knowing they would come.

The next thing I know I get a message through a friend who told me that potassium deficiency can cause dizziness and headaches. She told me that maybe I should try taking potassium the next time I was experiencing the anxiety/"going far away in my head" symptom. Within a week I read on line (on my very own message board no less) a conversation among IC patients talking about the potassium test. It turned into a conversation about whether or not we loose potassium in our urine and someone ended up posting an article written by Dr. Mirken about how vomiting and diarrhea cause potassium loss. And it hit me. I had been experiencing diarrhea with my anxiety for a long time now and I most likely did have a potassium deficiency. I remember how much better I was doing back when I took potassium the first time (shortly after healing my bladder) to help with the edema. At the time, even though I did notice it helping with the swelling, I think I attributed my doing better "on the whole" to the B vitamins, but it was probably a combination thing. Not to mention that both having sodium and potassium in balance and having enough B vitamins (especially B6) help prevent water retention/edema. Anyway, the very next day I "just happened" to clean off my desk so I could dust and get re-organized. I ended up coming across a note I had written over two years ago. My IC friend Janie was having trouble with dizziness and falling down. The doctors couldn't figure out what was wrong and she was having all kinds of tests done. I asked a medical intuitive I know about her just in case she had any insights that could help. Her response, which I had written down, was that Janie was deficient in potassium. Aside from the fact that it was totally weird of me to still have this note on my desk from two years ago, something I would normally have thrown away by now, I couldn't believe my eyes when I saw what I had written. Now whether she was right about Janie or not, I don't know, but I was shocked to see potassium deficiency discussed in relation to dizziness and light-headedness.

I decided to look it up in my alternative medicine books (of which now I have quite the collection) and found that potassium is a major healing mineral that works together with sodium to keep the acid/alkaline balance. That was the first thing I read and I thought how interesting that most IC patients have a very acidic body. I also thought it interesting that IC patients are often told to avoid foods high in potassium because they might irritate the bladder and how there are many IC patients who have IBS with diarrhea that might be loosing potassium along with their having a decreased supply in their diet. Anyway, I went on to read that potassium also helps calm the nerves and clear lymph gland congestion, both of which I knew I needed. And I was surprised to read (though at this point I have no idea why) that potassium also helps with the normal functioning of the adrenal glands. And if these connections weren't enough, I suddenly remembered reading that one of the roles of progesterone in the body is to help keep potassium and magnesium in the cells. As I was increasing my progesterone level, I believe it caused my body to crave more potassium. Confirmation of that came when I had two or three very high sodium meals in a row and it made me very sick and gave me that "going far away in the head" feeling along with diarrhea and more anxiety feelings. No wonder the "going far away in the head" feeling didn't seem to be getting better, even though the progesterone cream seemed to be helping me in so many other ways. And I thought, maybe that is also why I got the acid reflux and acid stomach back when I first started increasing my progesterone level. Anyway, by the time I read that calcium deficiency and potassium deficiency both promote panic attacks, I was beside myself. Again I was amazed at all the connections *and* at all the signs that had led me to them. Again God was showing me the answers. And again, it was time for me to take action.

I decided to start taking a calcium/magnesium supplement (even though the Noni juice has a fairly good supply) along with a potassium supplement each day and it has made a huge difference. I decided to increase the amount of Noni I was drinking to help cleanse my colon and rebuild my body. I also decided to get back to bouncing on the rebounder (i.e., mini-trampoline). I had been slacking off on that and really I shouldn't have been. It was so important to cleaning out my lymph glands and I should not have stopped doing it. There was a time when my neck and shoulder were hurting so much that it hurt to bounce and so I stopped doing it for a while and never went back. Clothes and stuff had piled up on the rebounder (which we keep in the corner of the bedroom). I cleaned everything off it the day I figured this out and have been bouncing every day since. Immediately my swelling started to go down. I knew this wouldn't be near as bad as when I had to cleanse before because I'm not near as toxic as I was when my IC was severe. But I also knew it wouldn't happen overnight. I felt like I had to re-commit myself to healing all over again. I had to re-commit myself to taking extra good care of myself, something of which, as I've said, I've never been all that good at doing. But I was going to do it. If it was going to get me better and give me my life back, then I was going to do it.

Just like with my IC, and really all of my IC related symptoms, I found that there were multiple causes on multiple levels for my anxiety/fear. On a physical level, the anxiety/fear was being caused by an imbalance in my hormones and a deficiency in B vitamins. It was also being caused by an exhausted nervous system and exhausted adrenal glands. And last, but certainly not least, it was being caused by toxicity and a potassium deficiency that gave me that feeling like I was "going far away in my head". On a psychological level, my anxiety/fear was being caused by thoughts and memories of bad experiences I had when my IC was severe combined with the still very real unpredictable physical risk of getting horribly sick. On an emotional level, I can look at the anxiety/fear that has been coming out the past couple years as fear that I couldn't release back when I was sick. It was all so overwhelming that it was just way too much to feel back then. It was too big. And my adrenaline and determination to heal wouldn't allow it. It's like in some way the fear is just now catching up with the physical. I think it would have been unnatural for it to never come out. And on a spiritual level, it was my lack of faith that I would be okay that caused me to be afraid. I knew it would help me heal faster and more completely if I addressed the symptom on every level. That's how I did it for all of my other IC and IC related symptoms and it always helped.

So even though the natural progesterone cream was helping me, alone, it just wasn't enough. It wasn't some magic cream in a jar that was going to get rid of all of my remaining symptoms as I had hoped. Just like there is no magic pill to heal from IC, there was to be no magic "pill" for me to fix my remaining symptoms either. Like with my bladder, there were several different causes that I had to address before I could get better. It was never just one thing that I did that got me better. It was the combination of things I did. And it was to be that way with the anxiety and my remaining symptoms as well. Just like it took a combination of things to make me sick, it took a combination of things to get me well.

The combination of the natural progesterone (i.e., rebalancing my

148

hormones), taking a natural potassium supplement (i.e., rebalancing my sodium/potassium balance), taking a natural calcium/magnesium supplement (to help my nerves and fix my deficiency in both), increased amounts of Tahitian Noni (to help cleanse and rebuild) with an occasional Colostrum (to help boost my immune system and help cleanse), bouncing on the rebounder (to help cleanse my lymph glands and strengthen my internal organs), and getting back on B vitamins (to help my nervous system and everything else) are *all together* what's helping my remaining symptoms. Because these things are helping my physical symptoms to no longer occur, there will no longer be a need to be psychologically afraid or nervous which should further aid my adrenal glands and nervous system in healing the rest of the way.

The last part of me getting back to normal, I know, has to do with stress. Ironically, the stress of this book (not the actual writing of it, but the worrying whether I'm doing a good enough job or whether it will help people) was adding to my remaining symptoms by putting an extra strain on my body. On many levels, it's time for me to let it all go...the swelling, the poison, the memories, and the stress. It's time for me to take my own advice and to again start paying attention to the needs of my body.

"The body cannot be cured
without regard for the soul."
- Socrates

Chapter 11

Healing the IC
Body, Mind, and Spirit

It wasn't my fault that I got sick just because *now* I could see how it happened. And it wasn't my fault that I got sick just because *now* I could see the possible emotional and spiritual reasons involved. It didn't make my physical symptoms any less real. It didn't make my IC (or all that came with it) "an emotional illness" or a disease caused by my psyche. IC is a very physical disease, just like cancer and diabetes are very physical diseases. But it doesn't mean that there aren't emotional and spiritual reasons for why people get cancer and diabetes. (Of course there are.) Just because I was recognizing the connection between my mind, body, and spirit, didn't mean that I stopped recognizing the many physical causes. And just because I began to understand the messages my spirit was sending me through my body, did not mean that I could stop treating my symptoms on a physical level either. In fact, I could never have gotten better otherwise. But just as I believe that addressing our whole body together as a unit, versus only our bladder, gives us a better chance of healing from IC, I also believe that addressing the body, mind, and spirit together gives us an advantage toward healing faster, more fully, and more permanently.

What I have learned healing from IC is that there are so many tools at our disposal on every level. Things we can do for our body, our mind, and our spirit that can help us to heal. There is truly no reason to feel discouraged when we realize that we have a very strong healing power inside of us that is available to us at all times. A healing power so strong that even doctors can be shocked to see their patients heal "against all odds". We have inside of us, each one of us, a healing power so strong that it can literally heal an "incurable" illness. And we also have a healing power available to us always through God/the Universe that can help us the whole way through.

In recognizing the connection between our mind, body, and spirit and taking responsibility for the health of our *entire* being, we are taking back some control. And taking back some control after getting a disease that we had no control over getting, a disease where we have no control over what's happening to our body, a disease where we are constantly told that there is no cure, is a *really big deal*. Not only will we be taking control of our physical health (which is extraordinarily important with a disease like IC), but also of our happiness, our emotional well being, and (not to be overly dramatic, but...) our very life. In recognizing the connection and using the connection, we are, in a very real sense, taking our power back. We are making a statement to ourselves and to the universe that we have the power to help heal ourselves, that we have the power to make changes in our lives, and that we have the power to make choices that can help us do both. As I said earlier, the mind/body/spirit connection is not about blame. It's about power.

I know some people think of the mind/body/spirit connection and automatically think of things like crystals, "new age" thought and alternative treatments. And sure you can use crystals, alternative treatments and be "into" new age thought, but you most certainly don't have to. It doesn't matter whether you choose to take synthetic medications or have medical procedures done to treat your IC, or whether you choose to detoxify your body with natural treatments and use acupuncture, for example, to treat your IC. You can still utilize the connection between your mind, body, and spirit to help you heal regardless of how you are treating your IC on a physical level. And you don't have to believe what some people call "new age" thought in order to use the connection either. You can be Christian, Buddhist, Jewish, or Hindu and it makes no difference. It makes no difference whether you believe that there is no such thing as a coincidence (in other words, everything happens for a reason) or that everything happens haphazardly. And it doesn't matter whether you understand the emotional and spiritual reasons behind your IC right now, or for that matter, ever. In fact, you can believe that your emotions and spirit had *absolutely nothing* to do with your getting sick and *still* you can use the connection between your mind, body, and spirit to help you get better.

Really, all you need recognize is that we are made of energy. We are energy beings and we are made of the same energy (or stuff) that everything in the universe is made of. Believing or recognizing that we are made of energy and so is everything else, is not all that difficult when we realize that these are physical facts. This is quantum physics, all concepts that can be proven scientifically. In fact, not only are scientists and doctors aware that we are made of energy (and that we are, in fact, electrical beings) they are also aware of the power of our mind and thoughts in healing our body through what they call the placebo effect. If someone takes a sugar pill but believes it to be medicine, it can work the same way as it does for someone who is taking the actual medicine. Even biofeedback, which has recently gained popularity in mainstream medicine, is a reflection of the power of our mind in healing our body. Because we are energy beings and because our thoughts are made of energy, we are able to affect our healing with our thoughts.

Remember that all healing, whether through a surgical procedure or a Reiki healing session for example, is the transfer and the alteration of energy. Energy can be transferred in the form of thoughts, touch, ingested material, intention, desire and will. Our ability to effect energy is intrinsic because not only are we *made* of energy, we are also interconnected with all the energy in the universe. This is how we can, with our thoughts and intentions, help to bring healing to ourselves or to another. This is why positive healing affirmations can help us to heal.

An affirmation is a positive statement expressed in the present tense. An affirmation usually begins with "I am..." or "I see myself...". You fill in the blank with whatever it is that you desire for yourself in your future. For example, "I see myself as healthy and happy." Or "I am healing. I am healed." Or "I see my bladder healthy and strong." It is not a lie if while you are sick you are saying "I am whole. I am healthy." Affirmations are not facts of your current situation. They represent experiences that you desire. They are a tool of creation. The power of the word and the power of prayer are very similar in that you are sending out a request or an intention out to God/the Universe. We can speak and write affirmations and in this way we will be sending that particular energy out into the universe. The more you believe your affirmation and the more emotion you feel behind it, the more powerful it will be. It has been said that with faith the size of a mustard seed we can move mountains in our life. And we don't even have to have *blind* faith. Again, these principles are based on physics and on the laws of the universe. It is not some hocus-pocus. Where thoughts go, energy flows. We can use our words wisely, speaking of healing and thinking of ourselves as healing (or healed). We can pay attention to how we talk to our body and how we talk to ourselves. Instead of allowing negative thoughts to slow down our healing, we can use our thoughts to help us heal instead.

If we believe that we can't get well, if we believe that only remission is possible, we are already one step behind in creating a healthy bladder and body. If we don't believe that we can get well, it is much more likely that we won't. It's like if someone was playing a game thinking the whole time that they were going to lose. They will be much more likely to lose than the player who plays the game believing that he/she is going to win. If we speak and think of IC as if it is incurable, then that is the message we are sending to our body and out to the universe. And our body and the universe can do nothing but reflect that belief for us. If we believe we will get well, it will *literally* help us to get well.

Using the energy of our thoughts, beliefs, and words is only one way of using energy and the connection between our mind, body, and spirit. There are several ways to use energy to help us heal. Some examples are the energy of sound, color, relaxation, and love. All of these contain a vibration and can be used to help us heal. There are even "therapies" named after each one. Sound therapy, for example, can be as simple and profound as listening to music that you love that makes you feel happy or that makes you feel relaxed. Listening to the gentle sounds of the ocean, for example, can bring a sense of peace within the body. The relaxation response has actually been proven in scientific "mind-body" studies to help aid the body in healing. And really, it doesn't take a rocket scientist (as they say) to realize that anything that causes us to feel relaxed is going to help us heal. Even if you don't get into meditating, you can still do things that help you to relax. Whether it's listening to music, sitting in the quiet or in nature, taking a relaxing bath or even getting a massage, anything that helps us relax is going to be healing. I found that certain smells helped me to relax and feel better. I found champa scented and frankincense and myrrh scented natural incense both very relaxing and burned one of them often as I was taking herbal baths, meditating, or doing yoga. Lavender is considered a very relaxing scent as well. I used lavender oil in my herbal baths and had lavender scented lotion and candles. But these were just my favorite scents, it's much more important for you to use your favorites.

Like sound, colors also vibrate at different frequencies and can therefore also be used to help us heal. You can surround yourself with certain colors to help you relax and feel better. For example, green, in general, is considered a very healing color. Black is considered a color that absorbs negativity. You can use candles of various colors, color bath therapy; even the colors of the clothing that you wear can help affect your healing. There is much written on color therapy and sound therapy if you are at all interested, but it is not necessary that you learn all about them in order to use them either. Just using the colors and sound/music that you are attracted to will work just fine. And most likely you are doing this already. If not, making a conscious effort to surround yourself with things that make you feel better is always a good thing. What is important when using sound, color or even scent (i.e., aroma-therapy) is using whatever makes YOU feel good. You don't need a book or another person telling you what to use. Use whatever you are attracted to and remember that these are just more tools to help us heal. It's not like you can't heal from IC if you don't wear the right colors or smell the right scents. Wouldn't that be funny? But seriously, you can't do any of this "wrong". These things are just more ways to use energy to help us get better.

One of the most powerful forms of energy we can use to heal is love. I know that many people don't think of sending love to their bladder. Most IC patients I talk to say things like they hate their bladder. They blame their bladder for being defective or sick. I have one friend, who has asked her family to remove her bladder after she dies and stomp all over it. Then she wants them to light it on fire and stomp on it some more. She hates her bladder thinking it's her bladders fault that she has gone through the misery of IC. Many people feel this way. But if, instead, they would send LOVE to their bladders, instead of anger, blame, and hate, it would actually help their bladder to heal.

If it's true that our body (and every cell in it) respond to what we think, feel, and say, then I would think it wise to send love instead of hate to our bladder. Just as plants have been proven to respond to loving words by growing stronger and healthier, while words of anger and hatred cause them to wilt and die, so does our bladder and body respond to what they are hearing. We can send love through our thoughts and through our actions. For example, we can support our bladder as it's trying to heal itself with soothing, non-toxic, natural things that won't harm the body in other ways. We can prevent certain things that we know will cause it further harm. We can love our bladder through all the pain and symptoms knowing that it is going through all of this *with* us (our mind and spirit) instead of looking at it as if it's *doing it to us*.

Most importantly, (and most obviously) we need to use energy on a physical level. We have to physically do things to help us heal. And if you have a more severe case of IC, I'm sorry to say, you may have to do a lot of different things like I had to. But the cool thing is, *you can do it*. And there are dozens and dozens of things you can try in order to discover what will work for you in your situation. (This is what my first two books are all about.) There is so much hope for you to heal regardless of your current situation or how long you have had IC.

Now naturally I don't expect everyone to share in my perspective of what I think IC is about or how to heal from it on any level. We are all different in our symptoms. We all have different causal factors and different connections between them. None of us will have the same exact healing path. We have to heal from IC the way *we believe* we have to heal. We have to try things that feel right to us, and for us, based on our own beliefs and our own individual symptoms. As I've said in my first two books, the specific things I did to heal from IC will not be the specific answers for everyone. But it's *the approach*, not the specifics, which has helped so many people since my first two books came out. And it is the approach I share with you here again (albeit briefly) because I still very much believe that by taking a similar approach, it truly IS possible to heal from IC.

It certainly wasn't luck that I got better from a severe case of IC and all the horrible symptoms that came with it. I had to do a lot of work and put forth a lot of effort. And it certainly wasn't genius that I got better because I'm certainly no genius. What I did, in general, was go back to the basics.

1. The body works together as a whole.
2. The body works always to heal itself.
3. The body needs good nutrition.
4. The body needs exercise to help cleanse itself and to keep everything running smoothly.
5. The body needs to REST.
6. The body cannot be constantly exposed to poison without being cleansed. It can only take so much.
7. Everything in nature seeks to find balance.

159

Based on the premise that my body was already trying to heal itself, I used all things that *supported* my body versus things that my body had to "fight" or "recover from". That was very important in my healing and, I feel, a big downfall of the medical approach. The poking, prodding, stretching, dyes, and synthetic medications often work against the body's natural healing tendencies and cause the body more stress, more toxicity, more to process, and more to recover from. I know this might sound strange to some people, but to be perfectly honest, I felt I was literally too sick to take the medical approach. I believe it would have just about killed me to do some of those things. But that was just the way it was for me. Again, I know there are some people who find relief in the medical treatments and as you know, I am for anything that helps an IC patient find relief from their symptoms. But for me, I went the whole other way. I used things that were very gentle and tried not to put any more strain on my body than was absolutely necessary as I attempted to cleanse all the poison out of me and rebalance my body.

In order to heal from IC I had to change the environment in my body. I had to remove every source of toxin/poison that I could think of and cleanse my body. Like most people with IC, I was *very* sensitive so I had to be extremely careful with everything I took and everything I did. Whenever I didn't, it was nearly always a mistake that resulted in an increase in my symptoms. I cleansed gently and slowly because that was all my bladder and body could tolerate. The faster I tried to go, the stronger the stuff I took to cleanse, the more my symptoms increased. I had to adjust how fast I was cleansing based on how I was feeling. And I had to soothe my insides while I cleansed. I had to soothe the inflamed, irritated, burning tissues in my bladder with soothing, healing, non-toxic, gentle things like marshmallow root tea for example. This was very important. Providing soothing support that was nutritive to the tissues made a big difference in healing my bladder. And by changing the environment within my body to a less toxic one, I was also making it less conducive to bacteria, fungus, and viruses. By removing the toxicity and soothing the whole way through, I helped reduce the inflammation and irritation to the tissues and helped them to heal.

Once I got sick and was so toxic and out of balance, I couldn't tolerate the things I needed in order to get well. My bladder couldn't handle it and, for that matter, neither could the rest of my body. I couldn't take the vitamins and minerals that I was lacking or eat things that were healthy because it caused my bladder more pain and more symptoms. This is a big part of the problem with healing from IC. *We need the things that we can't tolerate.* In order to get better, we need to get our bladder and body to the point where we can tolerate the things it needs. B vitamins are the perfect example. As much as my body needed them, they burned and hurt my bladder so much that I couldn't take them. This is how it is for most IC patients with B vitamins, vitamin C, potassium, and all kinds of other supplements (depending on the person). But in order to heal from IC and all the other symptoms that came with it, I knew I had to rebuild my body. I had to nourish it with the vitamins, minerals, amino acids (protein), and enzymes it needed to heal. So I had to determine what I was deficient in and find a way to get it into my body without hurting my bladder in the process. This wasn't always easy. This is why I used liquids such as single herbs in tea form, protein or nutrition drinks, and wheatgrass juice, for example, because this way I could take very small amounts. And in taking small amounts I was at least able to get some nutrition into my body to help it heal. As I continued to remove the sources of toxicity (e.g., cigarette smoking, mercury amalgam, yeast) and continued to cleanse and soothe my insides, I was eventually able to tolerate more and more.

To heal from IC I had to bring my body back into balance. I used natural things like acidophilus (which is the active culture in yogurt and already exists in our bodies) to rebalance the intestinal flora, good nutrition and natural supplements (as much as my bladder and body could tolerate of course) to fix deficiencies and give my body what it needed to heal. Once my bladder could handle it, I used things like protein drinks, liquid minerals, wheatgrass juice, and Tahitian Noni, to help rebuild my body. I used NAET, acupressure and reflexology (all of which are completely painless ways to help release blockages, cleanse, and re-balance the body), along with things like yoga, exercise, and meditation. Another major way I found balance in my body, in the end, was by rebalancing my hormones. I learned that they were affecting most all of my symptoms, from the hypothyroidism to the IBS, the fibromyalgia to the IC. I believe it was the first thing for me that got out of balance and if I would have known then what I know now, it is probably where I would have started in terms of trying to heal.

To heal from IC I had to find balance not just in my body, but in my life as well. I had to get rid of toxic people and toxic situations. A toxic person is someone with negative energy, someone who mistreats us, someone who takes energy from us and doesn't give back, someone who generally leaves us feeling bad one way or the other. A toxic situation is one in which we are being used, abused, taken advantage of, or surrounded by negative energy. In order to heal, I had to get away from all of that. I had to stop allowing other people to mistreat me. I had to identify what and who was draining my energy and put a stop to it. I needed my energy to heal. I needed to be away from the poison and the bad feelings. And I needed to be away from the source of both. I had to release bad habits and painful emotions, both of which were toxic to my body.

So as I cleansed my body, I was also cleansing my emotions and cleaning out my life. The things that came up to be healed were often painful things, sometimes ugly things, things that I didn't want to face or admit to myself. There were things I felt guilty about, things I felt insanely sad about, and things I felt totally ashamed of. It wasn't fun to acknowledge these things, but I felt I had no choice. I knew had to face them in order to get through them. I had to face them to be able to release them. I knew that the solution was not to block the pain or cover it up, but to heal it. I wanted to get to the root of the problem on every level, not just on a physical level, because I knew that it all goes together. And so I looked. I examined. I cried. And I felt horrible. But just for a time. Time enough to heal my emotions and my spirit. Time enough to find a way to let it all go.

But at first I had no idea how to let it all go. I had no idea how to stop being angry or stop feeling hurt, especially about the stuff that was still happening. For example, at first I dealt with my hurt feelings and anger at the people who didn't care or believe me when I got IC by moving to the other side of town so I wouldn't see them and by not talking to them anymore. But eventually I realized that it didn't matter whether I saw them or spoke to them ever again. It was my own feelings that I needed to "get away from". They most likely didn't even know how I was feeling and I certainly wasn't "punishing" them by not seeing them or talking to them. Not that I wanted to "punish" them, but I did wish for them to be aware of how very real IC is, of how uncaring they had been, and how upset I was about it. But I'm quite sure they never gave it a thought. The problem was, that I did. I thought about it and felt bad about it a lot. And I didn't want to. I didn't want to care what they thought and I didn't want to care that they didn't care. But I didn't know how to feel better. I sat alone, sick and in pain, for months and months, feeling bad about the fact that no one cared that I was sitting alone, sick and in pain, for months and months.

Along with feeling sorry for myself (and blaming myself) for no one caring that I was suffering so much physically, I admit I was also angry. As I said earlier, it's a lot easier to feel angry than it is to feel hurt. It's less painful and also easier to release, especially initially. It's also easier to express anger with someone close to us; someone who we know loves us and we know will forgive us. For me, that person was my mom. When I was first real sick, I was especially angry with my mom. Not only because she was still talking to all those people I moved away from, but because I wanted her to help me. Initially I wanted her to help me find a doctor and help me do some research. I was much too sick to be doing either. But mostly I wanted her to understand how hard it was for me to be *that* sick and have no one seem to care. I wanted her to stick up for me. I wanted her to explain to my relatives and to others (only when they asked about me of course) that I *really was sick*. That just because they couldn't figure out what was wrong with me for nearly a year did NOT mean that I was crazy or that it was "all in my head". I wanted her to yell at the people that were horrible to me, not be friends with them. She kept telling me that she wanted me to let go of my anger at them for not caring about me so that I could get better. But I couldn't. And at the time, I didn't feel I should have to. I felt very justified in staying angry. And besides, to be perfectly honest, I didn't know *how* to stop feeling bad about it.

We will always have "stuff" to let go of in our lives. And some of us are going to be better at it than others. Some of us can let things and feelings flow through us and then flow right out. Others of us hold onto them and let them fester. We think about what happened, feel it again, and think about it some more. And maybe we're not thinking about it consciously all the time, but when it comes back up, we end up feeling the same way about it no matter how much time has passed. We just have trouble letting it go. That's how it was for me. Being a sensitive type of person, sometimes, instead of letting things roll off my back, I would allow my feelings to be hurt. And sometimes, I would have trouble "forgetting about it". I would forget for a time, but then when something came up that reminded me about it again, I would feel bad about it all over again. When things happen that hurt us deeply, it can be much more difficult to let them go. That's how it was for me when it came to certain people not believing or caring that I was in so much pain and so sick with IC. I keep using this as an example because I think this happens to so many IC patients and if it happened (or is happening) to you, I want you to know that you're not alone. Because really it can be shocking and quite devastating to those of us who would never have expected this type of response from family and friends. Like myself, I never could have imagined that I could be in the hospital four times (once out of state), have three surgeries, almost die twice, and not have a single person from my family or friends call or say boo about it. To be honest, I felt pretty stupid for ever thinking any of them cared to begin with. And as I said, I felt like there must be something terribly wrong with me that this could happen. I felt embarrassed to Charlie (not that it was necessary because he didn't (and doesn't) care what anyone else thinks of me, he still loves me the same). But still, I did feel embarrassed and I guess, also very sad. This was probably the meanest thing that "other people" have ever done to me. From that perspective, I guess I should be happy. A lot of people have to suffer MUCH more at the hands of others than I ever had. This was just a lack of concern and compassion with a little bit of "they think I'm nuts" thrown in. But I'll tell you, it was so incredibly hurtful that it was hard for me to get over it all at once. It was definitely a process that took some time.

Sometimes it's difficult to let go of really big emotional pain just because it's hard to face it all at once. It was like that for me when my dad died. As I said earlier, I couldn't feel it all at once. I could only handle it in very small pieces. So I *had* to hold onto it. I had no choice but to hold onto it because we have to feel something before we can let it go and I couldn't do that all the way. The hurt was too much for my body to handle when I was sick. I could literally only cry for a few short minutes before I would get physically sick from crying. I would get so congested I could barely breathe. I would start choking and coughing, my stomach would get in a knot and I would start shaking all over. My bladder would spasm, hurt more, and sometimes stop working all together. I would have to force myself to stop crying and think about something else. I was just too sick to cry that hard. So I would do things like cry at stupid television shows or movies instead of facing my own personal emotional pain of missing my dad because it was much easier to let things out like that, little by little. And sometimes it's like that releasing emotional pain where we can only do it a little bit at a time.

Learning to release emotional pain was a big part of my healing. But just like healing physically, it took time for me to heal my emotions. First I had to understand my feelings and what was causing them. As I explained earlier, the symbols pointed me in the direction of things to consider but it still took self-examination before I could understand what they meant for me. Once I identified the hurt, the fear, the anger, etc. and understood where it came from, I had to figure out to heal it. That was definitely the harder part for me. One of the ways I did that (before I really understood *how* to) was just to feel the feelings and talk about them. I got angry and yelled. I felt hurt and cried. I talked to Charlie about everything and he was wonderful and patient and understanding. He allowed me to have feelings and to share them with him. He didn't judge me or make fun of me or make me feel stupid for feeling how I felt. It's important to have someone that we can do this with. If we don't have someone close to us, like a spouse or friend, then it's important to find *someone*. Other IC patients can be very helpful to each other in this way. But regardless of whom we share our feelings with, whether a spouse, minister, friend, family member, or another IC patient, I believe the important thing is to get these feelings out of us. I believe that it's healthier than keeping them in. I think many of us keep them in because we think it's "wrong" to be angry or unbecoming to yell and scream. Or maybe we are too embarrassed to even admit we feel hurt or to not act like we are fine. That's how I had always been. But with IC, I began to allow myself the time and privilege of feeling the way I felt. Even though it is important to be calm and relaxed in order to heal, I believe we still also need to release the negative emotions that are adding more stress and draining our body of much needed energy.

Physical pain, when remembered, is not physically felt. But emotional pain, when remembered, can hurt exactly the same. In fact, sometimes it can hurt even worse when we remember something because when we re-think it, we might have a new insight and become even more hurt by it. We can be hurt multiple times by the same exact thing simply by remembering it and thinking about it. That's why it is so important to heal the emotional hurts. Otherwise they can continue to hurt us.

Once I began looking at things from the perspective of energy, I started to understand more about how to let go of hurt feelings and negative emotions. I learned that by remembering everything in our lives that went wrong or hurt us, we are, in those moments, re-creating that same energy around us once again. Sadly, when we look at our own past actions (or at another's past and sometimes present actions), we often judge and criticize. And in those moments of looking at another (or ourselves) as "bad" or "evil", we are actually calling to ourselves the energetic vibrations of those actions or thoughts. In other words, as we judge another, whether the judgment is justified or not, we are still lowering our own vibration. We are still drawing the energy or the essence of that judgment to ourselves. And as we remember "bad" things that happened to us, we also draw the energy of that "bad" thing to us all over again.

So eventually I came to realize that, as usual, my mom was right. Holding on to the anger and not forgiving people that had hurt me, really could affect my healing from IC. Recreating the emotional pain every time I thought about it was only adding more stress to my body. But how was I going to stop feeling bad about something that was still happening? And how was I going to forgive them for hurting my feelings *this* much?

What I came to learn is that forgiveness is a choice, just as not forgiving is a choice. And like everything else in the universe, forgiveness is also a process of transferring energy. When there is someone in our life that we think we can't forgive we should remember this...the energy of that person and/or situation remains within our aura (or our energy field). When we can't forgive another, we remain, energetically speaking, connected to that person. We are choosing, in a sense, to allow the pain, abuse, or whatever happened, to remain with us. So choosing not to forgive someone for a wrong they did to us is really choosing to allow that person or situation to bother and affect us for the rest of our life. We sort of "carry" it with us even if we aren't consciously thinking about it. We need to forgive them, then, for our own sake. Forgiveness, I've learned, has much more to do with being nice to ourselves than to those we are forgiving. It's funny because I used to think of forgiveness as something we sort of "grant" to another person. I also used to think that it automatically implied that "it's okay" whatever it was that they did. But now I understand it as something else entirely.

Now I understand that forgiveness is not to say that it is all right that someone hurt us, but to recognize that holding onto the anger and hurt feelings is only hurting us more. What they did to us can remain as "wrong" or as "evil" today as it was when they did it, but if we forgive them, we can release the energy surrounding what they did. We can cleanse our energy field of the negativity and we can release the emotions that we have attached to "it" or "them". Our emotions carry a lot of energy. They are the energy behind our thoughts that can give them so much power. And if we are carrying negative emotions, even if it is only subconsciously, we are drawing more negativity to us. We need to let things go so that they don't affect us anymore. Forgiveness of others can, in this way, be seen as an act of self-love.

So in the end, again, I had to do something that I wasn't very good at. I had to be nice to myself. I had to care enough about myself to not want to carry the hurt and angry feelings with me anymore. Because even if I wasn't consciously thinking about them, they were obviously still there or I wouldn't have felt upset whenever something came up about it. I had to care enough about myself to choose to forgive them for hurting me. I had to remember that it wasn't about them at all. It was about me. It was about what I thought of myself and how I was treating myself. I knew that, on one level, they were just reflecting that for me anyway. And I had to stop being angry with them for not understanding how horrible it feels to be in the situation I was in with IC. They couldn't possibly relate or know how it felt unless something similar had happened to them. I chose to believe that they weren't intentionally trying to be hurtful to me. And eventually thinking these things did help me to forgive them.

But at first all I could do was *want* to forgive them because I knew it was the best thing for *me*. I knew I was never going to talk to them about it anyway. What I learned was that even when we find it near impossible to forgive someone because we feel so hurt/angry, we can still state our intention to God/the Universe that we are choosing to forgive even if we don't know exactly how we can. The intention and desire to forgive is all that is really needed. We need not even tell the person we are forgiving. We can do it all in our own heart. They need not know a thing about it. This is why it is still healing to forgive someone who has passed on. As long as we have the intention and desire, we can cleanse ourselves of the energy of other people (and situations) through forgiveness whether we end up gaining a perspective that makes us feel better about what happened or not.

The strange thing that happened to me was that in trying to forgive a person that hurt me, I ended up beginning the process of forgiving myself. I came to realize that it was no coincidence that I was angry with my mom for the same reason that I was angry with myself. I was angry with myself for not sticking up for myself. It's interesting how often we find ourselves upset with somebody about something and then, if we stop to think about it (and are honest with ourselves about it) we end up realizing that it's really ourselves we are upset with about that same exact thing. It's just like how we criticize in others what we don't like about ourselves. It's the same kind of thing. Anyway, as I said earlier, there were many times before I was sick and even shortly thereafter, where I hadn't spoken up for myself. Times where I had allowed others to take advantage of me in some way or convince me to do things that didn't feel right to me in my gut. Once I realized that it was really me who I was upset with, it was much easier to let go of my anger at my mom. I was able to forgive my mom for not being exactly the way I wanted her to be. I mean, who is exactly the way we want them to be anyway? Besides, we can't expect from other people what we are not willing to give ourselves. And so...I started to stick up for myself. And I started to care a LOT less about the people who didn't care about me and instead started caring more about myself.

Part of my learning to care more about myself was finding a way to forgive myself. It was *much* more difficult for me to forgive myself than it was for me to forgive others. For one thing, I was much more angry with myself than I was with other people. And if any emotion such as anger had contributed to why I got sick in the first place, it was my anger with myself that was most likely for sure at the root of it. I had repeatedly hurt myself the ten years prior to getting sick by allowing other people to mistreat me and allowing them to make me feel bad about myself. I had been showing my feelings and my body very little respect the years prior to my getting sick. And I wasn't at all pleased with myself about any of it. It was my anger with myself that I really needed to get rid of to help me get better. I had to stop "beating myself up about it" as my dad used to say.

I remember reading somewhere that forgiveness of the self will hand you the key to the light of your soul. But how do we forgive ourselves? I'll tell you how. (Now that I've finally figured it out!) We have to show ourselves the same compassion and understanding that we would show a friend or loved one. So many of us have much more trouble forgiving ourselves than we do another. We tend to show more compassion and understanding to others and hold ourselves up to much greater scrutiny. But forgiving ourselves is one of the most healing things we can do. It helps us to release all kinds of negative emotions like shame, blame, anger, and hurt. Forgiving ourselves is an even greater act of self-love than forgiving others. Once we forgive ourselves we stop sending thoughts of hatred, anger, and disappointment to our body (and ourselves) and instead replace it with compassion, understanding, and self-acceptance. This makes for a much healthier body, mind, and spirit.

Once we are able to release negative and painful emotions through forgiveness (of ourselves and others) we will have more energy available to help us heal. We might not even realize how much of our energy was tied up with these emotions until we release them. Just as we may not even be aware of how often our thoughts of ourselves are negative or how much other people are draining our energy until we put a stop to it. When we begin to notice where we are putting our energy, where we are losing our energy, and who in our life is "sucking" our energy, we can have more control of our energy level and thus also, our health and well being.

Becoming aware of our thoughts and where we are putting our energy, where we are losing our energy, or how we are using our energy to create our life is what awakening is about. It's about the power of self-awareness and using this awareness to help us heal. This is truly what the mind/body/spirit connection was all about for me. For me, it was about recognizing that I actually did have some control. And that just because I did, it didn't mean that it was my fault that I had gotten sick in the first place. For me, it was about recognizing that there really was a connection between what was happening to me physically and what was going on inside of me. And that didn't make me a bad person or an inept person. It didn't mean that I was thinking "wrong" or acting "wrong" and it didn't mean that I was weak. It didn't mean that I had committed some unforgivable sin and was being "punished". And it didn't mean that I was less of a person than someone who is healthy. We all (even non-IC patients) get sick at times. We all have emotional pain. We all think negative thoughts. After all, we are all only human. What I've come to understand is that when we are out of balance in our emotions or when we are heading down a path that is not particularly good for our spirit, sometimes our body responds. I've learned that even when we aren't conscious of how we are feeling, it can still affect our health. And even when we aren't aware of how we are thinking, speaking, and acting, simply because we aren't paying attention to how we are thinking, speaking, and acting, it can still affect our health. Once we become aware that there is a connection, once we realize that one thing does affect the other (our body can affect our mind and spirit, and our mind and spirit can affect our body) it offers us an opportunity to use that information to our advantage.

"You yourself, as much as anybody in the entire universe, deserve your love and affection."
– Buddha

Chapter 12

◆

The Spiritual Message of IC

Recognizing that I was angry and disappointed with myself for various reasons and that maybe that might have had something to do with why I got sick was one thing. I could see now that how I was feeling and thinking about myself might have affected me physically. I could even see how thinking subconsciously (and even sometimes consciously) for so long that there was "something wrong with me" might have had something to do with my getting sick. And of course now I could see all the different physical causal factors involved that explained, on a physical level, why I got sick. Yet still I had to wonder. Why IC? Why was it that I got IC and not some other disease? Why did I end up getting a disease that was so complicated, so difficult to diagnose and treat, and so difficult for doctors and other people to understand? This I didn't understand for a long time. But now I know. Now I know that I got IC for the same reason that any of us get any disease. I got IC because I needed the messages, lessons, and gifts it has to offer.

Sometimes bad things happen to us because we need their gifts. Of course when they first happen it's difficult to see what those gifts might be. When we first get sick it is much more difficult to see the gifts or to understand the messages. At first it is much more difficult to understand why this all happened to us on every level. Initially we have trouble seeing the physical causal factors involved in our IC because it's usually not at all obvious and also because there are usually multiple causes contributing to our symptoms. But as time goes on and we explore the different possibilities and try different treatment options, we begin to understand. Either through the process of elimination (of what's not working for us) or through learning about a possible contributing factor and getting tested for or trying to address that factor, we begin to unravel the IC mystery on a physical level. It is the same thing in terms of understanding why you have IC on a more emotional/spiritual level. It can be a process, it can take time, and it is not usually readily apparent. But understanding why you got sick with IC (on every level) can help you to heal.

It is not for me to tell you exactly how or why you got IC, not on a physical, emotional, or spiritual level. We are all different and there are most likely multiple reasons on every level for why you got sick. After all, it's always going to be a combination thing since everything is connected. But what I can tell you is this. The more symptoms and illnesses you have with your IC, the more reasons there probably are for why you are sick. And the more symptoms you have, the more severe they are, and the longer you've had them, I would say, the louder your body and spirit are trying to speak to you. Of course, it is totally up to you if you want to listen. I chose to "listen", as I've said, because I felt it offered me more opportunities to affect my healing. And I also chose to "listen" because it offered me a chance to understand "why me?" on a more emotional/spiritual level.

So how do we listen? How can we begin to understand the messages, lessons, and gifts that our IC has brought to us? We can begin by looking at the symbolic meaning of our symptoms and also in what it takes for us to heal.

Even though IC is here for different reasons for each one of us, I believe there are still some major messages that will probably apply to many of us. Because just as we have some things in common physically, it is most likely that we will also have some things in common emotionally and spiritually.

So why is IC here? What is it doing in our lives? Like most all illness, IC is here to slow us down. With IC, we are pretty much forced to slow down because so often we need to be right near a bathroom. IC limits our activities and pretty much every aspect of our lifestyle. Depending on how severe our IC, some of us are unable to work and some become housebound or even bedridden. Because we all have IC to different degrees, our bodies (and our IC) will be telling us to slow down to different degrees. Obviously the more severe your IC, the more your body is telling you that you need to slow down.

IC is also here to wake us up. Actually, I believe IC is a wake up call on every level. It is a call to society to look at what we are doing with all the synthetic hormones, artificial foods, pesticides, toxic chemicals, antibiotics, toxins, and pollutants. I believe that IC patients (and those with multiple chemical sensitivity (MCS) and other chronic, difficult to understand illnesses) are the "canaries in the coalmine" warning us of the risks that using all of these artificial, toxic poisons can produce. IC is a call to society for there to be a reduction of the subtle but consistent poisoning of its people. And just like the fact that more women die of heart attacks in this country simply because they are not believed in the emergency room, IC is also a call to society to wake up to the way women are treated when a medical doctor doesn't know what's wrong with them through "normal" medical testing. IC is a call to medical doctors to remember to listen to their patients, to believe their patients, and to be open to the fact that something can be physically wrong with someone even if they aren't easily able to see it. Just because they don't understand it, doesn't mean it doesn't exist. IC is also a wake up call to the mainstream medical community and the alternative medicine community to work together for the benefit of the patient. There is good and bad in both and the answers and cures to IC and all of these "newer" chronic conditions will be found *much* faster if the two would work together. And of course, IC is a wake up call to each one of us on a personal level. It is a message from our spirit and a message from our bodies to, among other things, start paying attention to what we are doing to (and putting into) our bodies, what we are doing with (and even who we are putting into) our lives.

IC is here to help us find balance in our body, in our emotions, and in our lives. How do we know this? Because the more we find balance in our body, emotions, and lives, the faster and easier it is to heal from IC. This is my belief and of course this was also my experience.

In fact, all the things I did to help me heal from IC can all be looked at on every level. As I removed the sources of toxicity to my body, I was also removing the sources of toxicity to my emotions and my spirit by removing myself from toxic situations and toxic people. As I cleansed my body, I was also cleansing my emotions and my spirit (or energy) through forgiveness and releasing emotional pain. As I soothed my bladder and insides with natural, non-toxic, healing things, I was also soothing my emotions and spirit with understanding and compassion. As I did everything slow and gentle in terms of cleansing my body and what I was taking to heal physically, I also had to go slow and be gentle with myself in terms of healing my emotions and spirit. Neither happened overnight and neither could be healed overnight. And as I found balance in my body, I was also finding balance in my emotions and in my life. In order to heal, I had to be nice to myself physically (not taking anything or doing anything harsh because I was sensitive) and I also had to learn to be nice to myself emotionally because I am a sensitive person.

After talking to thousands of IC patients over the past eight years, I find it interesting how there are certain common personality characteristics among us and how there are also common "issues" that many of us seem to face. Interestingly (though not too surprisingly) these common traits are reflected in our common symptoms. For example, being sensitive is a fairly common personality trait among IC patients. Most IC patients I've spoken with are sensitive, compassionate, and empathetic types of people. It's interesting (and not too surprising) that so many IC patients have multiple allergies and are sensitive to various medications, foods, drinks, vitamins, herbs, and things in the environment. For many of us, it is very symbolic of our personality.

178

And just like being sensitive physically makes taking things (i.e., medications, herbs, etc.) much more difficult and therefore makes healing much more difficult, being sensitive personality-wise can also be more difficult. Sensitive people can get their feelings hurt much more easily and much more deeply than others. We pick up on things that others don't, notice little nuances, tones of voice, or other signals from people that others might miss. When we lose ourselves or lose sight of who we are, when we lose that type of grounding, we can get much more easily caught up with other people's energy. We can be so empathetic that we can literally take on other people's pain along with our own. Being sensitive, we can get SO hurt emotionally (just as we can get SO hurt physically having IC), much more so than a person who is not so sensitive (or who doesn't have IC). And I believe that's why we can get SO angry because we can get SO hurt. Anger being the most commonly associated symbolic message of bladder problems, it makes perfect sense to me that most IC patients are sensitive people.

One of the main messages of IC, in my opinion, is not necessarily "anger" even though that is the most commonly associated symbolic message of bladder problems. I believe it has more to do with releasing painful and/or negative emotion and anger is only one of those emotions. Symbolically speaking, water, almost always represents emotion. For IC patients, it is difficult to release water (or urine) from the body. And therefore, symbolically speaking, it is difficult for us to release emotion. This does not mean that it is difficult for us to release *any* emotion at all as if we are stoic and unfeeling. But maybe some of the emotions we feel inside are so painful that we have the symptom of painful urination. Maybe there is so much emotion that needs to be released that it is overflowing and we have the symptom of incontinence. Maybe there is so much painful emotion that needs to be released that we need to release it frequently and urgently. It is interesting to look at our specific bladder symptoms and the specific messages that might apply to us.

179

And even though releasing painful and/or negative emotion would include releasing anger, it doesn't mean that every IC patient is going to find that they are angry. If you are wondering if you are angry, if you are wondering if that particular symbolic message applies to you even though you don't necessarily *feel* angry or *act* angry, what you can do is this. Look at your life and find what is hurting your spirit. Find what is hurting you. Is it someone else? Is it you? Is it a memory of a past experience? When you find where you are hurt, that is where you will most likely find your anger. That is, if you have any. Maybe your emotional pain has more to do with missing a loved one who has passed on. Or maybe you had some other tragic happening in your life that has brought you emotional pain. Maybe you have another negative emotion like maybe you are feeling guilty and/or ashamed of something and you haven't been able to forgive yourself. Maybe you feel all of these things and maybe you haven't been able to release these feelings yet. These are all things we would determine through self-examination. As I've said, looking at the symbolic meaning of our symptoms is just a starting point and from there we will all be a bit different.

Another common personality trait that is reflected in our symptoms is having difficulty letting things go or difficulty releasing things that we no longer need. This is a major message because many of us not only have difficulty releasing waste through our bladder, but through our intestines as well. Many IC patients also have IBS (Irritable Bowel Syndrome) or some other form of problem with their intestines. Having our eliminative organs affected by our illness (e.g., the bladder and intestines), symbolically speaking, would mean that we have difficulty in releasing ideas, people, or situations in our lives that are no longer needed (just as our body no longer needs the waste). Whether we have trouble letting go of people (maybe a spouse who is mistreating us for example) or trouble letting go of hurt feelings, past mistakes, or even an unfavorable work situation, we are not all going to be exactly the same. Just like with the bladder, there are different variations of intestinal symptoms. For example, constipation represents holding things in, where diarrhea represents fear. Even more specifically, you

180

can look to see if it is painful for you to release through the intestines or if you don't release often enough (constipation). Look to see if it is fear (diarrhea) that causes you to release or if it literally makes you sick to release (that's how it was for me). You might have all of these symptoms intermittently as many of us with IC do.

Though several IC and IC related symptoms symbolically represent anger, there are also many that represent releasing or "letting go". They are about fear and about us not feeling safe, not only in our own body and life, but also in expressing our emotional pain. For some of us, the lessons IC brought might include recognizing that it's okay to have feelings. It's okay to express our hurt and anger. We are worthy. Our feelings count. We count. For some of us, maybe it's about us loving ourselves enough to release things (and feelings) for our own good. I don't think it's necessarily that we are consciously holding onto things or consciously afraid of releasing them. But maybe we are afraid to even think about something because we are afraid to *feel* it. Maybe the pain is so big that we are afraid to even look at it. (At least that's how it was for me.) But unfortunately we need to look at it and feel it in order to release it.

So many IC patients wrote me after reading *To Wake In Tears* and told me that as soon as they read the part I wrote about how it's okay to cry, they instantly burst out crying. How many of us hold in our emotional pain? How many of us don't feel safe to release it or justified in releasing it to our loved ones? How many of us hold on to "it" simply because "it" is too painful to even think about? I know several people with IC who have said things like "I wonder if I got IC because I used to "hold it" so long". I wonder if they realize how symbolic that is. If you listen to yourself as you describe your symptoms and then look at them on a symbolic level, you will notice many connections and messages for yourself. Listen to your words as you describe how you feel about your IC and about how you are feeling physically. Then take a look at your words and description on a symbolic level. Here is where you will begin to find some of your own messages.

Eventually being able to face and admit my true feelings, feelings that I didn't even know I had and having a safe place to release those hurt feelings was what helped me on an emotional/spiritual level. The greatest gift of love that Charlie gives me every single day is that he cares about my feelings. I was finally with someone that I could safely share my feelings with without the fear that I would be ridiculed, laughed at, not listened to, not understood, or told that I was "crazy", that I was "imagining it" or that I was "just exaggerating". As soon as I walked away from my first marriage, out of respect for my own feelings, to protect myself from getting hurt further, I ended up attracting someone who had respect for my feelings. Especially being a sensitive person, I definitely should not have been with someone overly critical or controlling. It was hurting my feelings and was a source of poison/toxicity to my spirit.

Many people believe that holding on to painful emotions causes physical pain to manifest in the body. They believe that holding on to old hurts and/or having on-going present day hurts can both manifest as disease within the body. And once we already have a disease, it can perpetuate it or prevent us from being able to heal. Having our energy tied up with painful thoughts and feelings can put stress on our body and therefore inhibit our healing. Just as leaving the sources of toxicity in place on a physical level can make healing more difficult, leaving the sources of toxicity to our emotions (and spirit) in place can also make it more difficult.

What I learned from having IC is that if we allow toxic people into our lives, if we remain in toxic situations, we are mistreating ourselves. If we put other people's feelings before our own, caring more about hurting their feelings than we do about our own feelings getting hurt, we are mistreating ourselves. If we take care of others at the expense of our own body or our own emotional well-being, we are mistreating ourselves. IC is here to teach us to stop mistreating ourselves. It is here to help us learn to put ourselves first.

You know the expression, "you teach what you have to learn"? Well I never realized how true that statement really is. Even in everyday life if we stop to think after we offer someone advice, we would realize that *we* should be the one listening to that advice. Once I started paying attention and started listening to what I was saying to other people, the advice I was trying to offer them, I was amazed at how often it was the case that I should be taking that same advice. It is no coincidence that I have been writing books telling other IC patients that they need to be nice to themselves in order to help themselves heal from IC. I have said it in both of my books and I say it all the time when I speak with IC patients. It is the lesson and the message that I most needed to hear.

I believe the main spiritual message of IC is self-love. Self-love is a major message because that is what it takes to help us heal. We have to be nice to our bladder, to our body, and to our self. The more we provide soothing support to our bladder, the faster and easier it is to heal the inflammation and rawness. The more we provide soothing support to our body (to all the other organs, muscles, and joints, that are affected by our IC), the faster and easier it is to heal. And the more we provide soothing support to ourselves emotionally, the faster and easier it is to heal. Accepting ourselves, releasing guilt, forgiving ourselves and others, releasing blame and anger are all ways of loving ourselves and are all very healing things for us to do. Others loving us and supporting us emotionally is also invaluable. It can be such a tremendous help not only in and of itself, but also in helping us to learn to love ourselves.

Self-love is a message, a lesson, and in the end, the greatest gift I received from my IC. Through my IC, I finally started to learn what being nice to myself really means. It means taking care of myself in every way (my body, mind, and spirit). And it means loving all of me, not just parts. It means loving the not so perfect parts too.

I started to realize that *resting* was "being nice to myself", that taking the time to do yoga, exercise, and meditate was "being nice to myself". I started doing things that I had never done before. For example, when

Charlie goes out of town for work, instead of ordering a pizza or eating something little and lame for dinner, I now actually make myself a real meal. I take the time, spend the money, and spoil myself by making myself an entire meal with healthy food. It's funny how shocked and impressed with myself I was that I started doing that. I also started speaking up and asking people, when they called in the middle of my "taking care of myself", if I could call them back later, instead of always letting other people's schedules dictate my own. I started allowing myself time to relax and time to do things that I enjoyed. I think I felt guilty (still) in doing those things, as if I didn't deserve them or as if I should be doing other "more productive" things. But not anymore, now I know I deserve them. Not only do I deserve them, but I also *need* them. We all do. We deserve the time for ourselves. We deserve the time to relax and do things we enjoy. We deserve to put ourselves first and take care of ourselves. We don't just deserve it; we actually *need* it in order to heal.

With IC, it's even more important to be nice to yourself in the moment. IC can make us so miserable physically that it makes it all the more important to make ourselves as comfortable as possible. It's important for us to show ourselves compassion through all the pain and stop blaming ourselves for it. We need to take care of ourselves first and then later, when we are feeling better, we will be able to take care of others as well.

Healing just naturally begs us to make a commitment to ourselves. Many people look down on the notion of putting themselves first believing it to selfish, self-centered, and egotistical. If that is what bothers you, please know that in putting yourself first you are truly being the most giving to those in your life who you love and want to take care of. By getting well and staying well, we are helping the ones we love to not have to worry about us being sick. Besides when we get well (because of putting ourselves first) we will have much more to give.

Part of my finding balance in my life meant learning to take care of myself before taking care of others. I had always done it the other way around. What I learned having IC is that there must be a balance in service to others and service to self. I had to remember this even when trying to help other IC patients. There was a point where it was taking most of my time and energy trying to help others (even as I was trying to heal myself) where I was essentially jeopardizing my own health by putting out too much energy when I couldn't afford to. I had to slow down and remember to take care of myself too. If I didn't, I would not have been able to help anyone and I would probably still be sick.

As I was writing this book I realized that I still hadn't found balance yet, not in my body or in my life. I had made a lot of progress, but not enough. Here I was writing another book, stressing out about trying to get it done faster and worrying whether I was doing a good enough job, and I was neglecting myself in the process. I stopped working out for a while because it was making me too tired and then I wouldn't feel like writing. I stopped doing yoga for a while because I just didn't take the time to take a break and do it. Ironically, I allowed the stress of getting this book done to inhibit me from healing the rest of the way.

So again it is time for me to follow my own advice. It's time for me to be nice to myself and finally allow my body the time to rest and recover the rest of the way. As I finish the final chapter of this book I understand what the final message of the anxiety/fear symptom is for me. The anxiety was my body yelling at me to REST. And I need to listen. I need to stop writing now and put myself (and my healing) first. I need to take a serious rest from stress so that I can finally get back to living my life, so that I can finally get back to feeling like me. But first I would like to leave you with some final words of advice, from one IC patient to another. It's no coincidence that it's the same advice that I most needed to hear when I was sick.

Remember, as you go about your healing from IC, to take time for yourself. Take time to be still and listen. Listen to the wisdom of your higher self, listen to your gut feelings, and listen for the signs from God/the Universe. Take time to listen to your body. It will guide you to what it needs. Watch and listen for the signs and symbols in your life. They are there for everyone. And they too will lead you to the answers you need to heal. Once you ask the questions, you will begin to see the answers all around you. They will be presented to you through your own thoughts and words. They will come to you through conversations with others, through books, through "coincidences", and through your own gut feelings. They will come to you through the symbols in your body and in your life. So remember to take the time to be still and listen.

Remember to breathe. And while you are breathing and telling yourself over and over again (as I used to do) that you are going to be okay, if you feel like crying...do it! Let yourself cry and get all the pain out of you. Don't be like me. Don't feel stupid for feeling afraid. And don't feel silly for crying. You have every right to feel the way you do. IC is tough. It can be torturous and extremely scary. It can be relentless and unpredictable. It can change our life in major ways preventing us from being who we want to be and doing what we want (and need) to do. And in the meantime, for many of us, as we suffer, we are offered little in the way of compassion and understanding. It is only normal to feel depressed and discouraged at times. But let me tell you something. You *can* and you *will* get well. You really are going to be okay. It doesn't matter what doctor or person has told you that you weren't going to get well. Don't believe them. Choose not to believe them. Believe in yourself instead. Believe in the power you have inside of you, the God given power we all have inside of ourselves to heal our own body. Believe in that instead. Know that you have guidance available to you always through God/the Universe. And know that there are answers out there for you no matter what situation you are in with your IC right now.

Surround yourself with healing. Make everything in your life about healing. And yet, keep it simple. With IC, doing less, taking less, going

186

slow and being gentle are often the better ways, the more healing ways, to go. Be nice to your body. Remember that your body is already trying to heal itself. So treat it with gentleness and offer it support. In every aspect of your life, surround yourself with support. Surround yourself with compassionate, understanding people who not only claim to love you, but show you that they do by their actions. And this includes you. It's important to show yourself that you love yourself by taking care of your physical needs and comfort first, before you start doing for and caring for others.

Fill your mind with healing thoughts and affirmations of healing. Write your intentions to heal and speak your intentions to heal. Clear the poison from your body and your life. Heal the emotional hurts so they can no longer manifest in your physical body. Ask for healing. Wish for healing. Pray for healing. And then act as if you already have it. Thank God for your healing even before you are feeling healed. This will only draw healing to you faster. And remember to be grateful for every step along the way, no matter how small the physical improvement might be, because gratitude will just naturally (by the laws of nature) draw healing to you faster.

We can change our perspective of our IC through gratitude for the gifts it has brought to us. For example, maybe we gained a greater appreciation of our loved ones or learned who are real friends are. Maybe we learned to say "no" instead of always doing what others ask of us or maybe we learned to slow down and take it easy on ourselves. Maybe IC caused us to change career paths or change our marital situation and maybe in the end, it was for the best that we made these changes. Maybe IC gave us the opportunity to help other people and make ourselves feel good because of it. Maybe we can look at the changes we have made in our lives because of IC and find the good in them. Or maybe it's too early on for you and you are having trouble seeing any good at all from being sick with IC. That's okay and that's totally normal. But I do believe that with some time, you will begin to see your IC for what it means to you. And that's really all that's important. It doesn't matter what I think the messages of IC are or what gifts and lessons I received. What matters is what it means to you. As I said, don't let anyone (including me) tell you why you have IC. Only you can know that. And you will. With time, I know you will.

Just as we do not cause the sun to rise and set, we do not control everything that happens to us. But we do always have control over our response to what happens, our attitude and feelings about what happens. Our attitude, feelings, and thoughts about our IC *are* within our control. And we can choose to use them to help us to heal. The healing of our emotions is also within our control. It is something else we can choose to do, along with all the physical things, to help us heal. We can also choose to use our IC as an opportunity for self-awareness and spiritual growth. We can choose to see our IC through the eyes of our higher self and use that understanding to help us heal. We can also choose to have hope. Hope is the spark to our healing. And our belief that we will get well is the magnet pulling us forward. We can never allow others to take that hope and belief away. And we can't take it away from ourselves. We need that hope. We *need* to believe. We need that vision of wellness so that we can help to create it.

Some people believe that illness can be seen as a state of grace. The body volunteering to be the teacher, the vehicle of Divine grace, by showing us what we need to release, to forgive, and to love. To me, IC is here to help us release whatever emotional pain we have, to forgive ourselves, and most importantly, to love ourselves. It is here to help us learn to treat our body and our feelings with respect and love. And if we do these things, if we learn to love ourselves on every level, we will take leaps and bounds forward in healing.

And like the phoenix from the ashes, we will rise again and begin anew. Our lives changed for the better because of having had IC. But it helps to be open to accepting the gifts. It helps to be open to hearing the messages. And it helps to be willing to let it all go. Not the IC, we're all willing to let that go, and not the materials things in life, but the anger, the hurt, the sadness, and the pain. It helps to be willing to give that all up, to empty ourselves, to clean out our bodies, our emotions, and our lives of all the waste. And most of all, it helps to love ourselves. Even in the moment of our greatest misery, even as we accept some responsibility for (on some level) creating that misery, we have to be willing to love ourselves. Loving, accepting, and forgiving ourselves, are perhaps the greatest challenges in getting better. But it is in learning to love ourselves that we gain the strength to heal and to stand tall once again.

Bibliography

Atkins, Robert C. *Dr. Atkins' Vita-Nutrient Solution: Nature's Answer to Drugs*. New York, New York: Simon & Schuster, 1999.

Lee, John R., Hopkins, Virginia, and Hanley, Jesse L. *What Your Doctor May Not Tell You About Premenopause: Balance Your Hormones and Your Life from Thirty to Fifty*. New York, NY: Warner Books, 1999.

Tenney, Louise, M.H. *Health Handbook*. Pleasant Grove, Utah: Woodland Books, 1994.

Tenney, Louise, M.H. *The Encyclopedia of Natural Remedies*. Pleasant Grove, Utah: Woodland Publishing, Inc., 1995.

Sellman, Sherrill *Hormone Heresy: What Women Must Know About Their Hormones*. Australia, Get Well International, (Revised edition) 2000.

For more information or to contact the author please visit

http://www.ic-hope.com